Keys to Effective Discipline

A Parent's Guide to
Managing Difficult Behavior

Ages 4 to 12

David A. Kilpatrick, Ph.D.

Casey & Kirsch Publishers
P.O. Box 2413
Syracuse, NY 13220

Keys to Effective Discipline
A Parent's Guide to Managing Difficult Behavior
Revised Edition

Copyright © 1992, 1995 By David A. Kilpatrick.

This book appeared in the first two printings under the title *Effective Discipline for Parents.* This current edition reflects numerous revisions to the original. The title change was made to be consistent with the *Keys to Effective Discipline* videotape, which is frequently marketed together with this volume.

First Printing . . . August, 1992
Sixth Printing . . .August, 1996

Published by:
Casey & Kirsch Publishers
P.O. Box 2413 Syracuse, NY 13220
(800) 331-5397

ISBN: 0-9646903-0-6

PRINTED IN THE UNITED STATES OF AMERICA

Contents

The Effective Discipline Approach

Other Issues in Discipline

Extra Helps

Chapter 1

So What's the Problem?

Most agree that raising children is a challenge. Many things make parenting more difficult these days. Single parent families, step families, families with both parents working, long work hours, financial problems, and marital tensions can all affect our ability to parent. The pressure on our children to do drugs, drink, or get involved with other undesirable activities is a major concern. Television feeds our children a steady diet of violence, sex, lying, and disrespect of parents. Parenting has never been easy, but today it seems tougher than ever.

Is raising children different than you expected? Maybe you pictured going on picnics, teaching your child to ride a bike, or reading stories together. Instead, you find yourself in an ongoing battle over all sorts of things. Our kids seem to challenge our words and frequently argue with us.

You already know the bad news: kids were not born with a manual. The good news is that much of the stress and conflict surrounding discipline is avoidable! There are a variety of ways to make discipline work in your home. Any parent can reduce the regular battle surrounding behavior and discipline by following the principles presented in this book. But you must be willing to take the initiative. Let's face it. Your child will never approach you and say "Mom (or Dad), I've been misbehaving too much lately. I've worked out a plan to curb my bad habits." *You* must be the one to take the initiative!

New and Improved Ideas?

The information in this book will help you learn how to be more effective at getting your children to behave. But the ideas presented are not new. In today's world of constant progress, we value what is new, what is "the latest." However, when it comes to parenting practices, anything new — no matter how clever it sounds — is by nature untested and not yet validated. Do you want your children to be guinea pigs for the latest parenting fad?

The fact that this book does not present "new" ideas is really a strength. The ideas on these pages are derived from behavioral principles which have been researched for over 50 years by hundreds of psychologists. In addition, these ideas have been used by thousands of families, while some of these practices have been in use for centuries. Psychologists have simply tested practices and ideas parents already use. With research, we can determine what works, why it works, and under what conditions various ideas are most helpful.

Even though many of the ideas have been around for awhile, many parents today are either unfamiliar with them, or they are unaware of the important behavioral principles which can make these ideas work. In the following chapters, you are going to learn dozens of approaches that will help in a variety of situations. More importantly, you will learn how to make any strategy more effective.

Will This Work With Your Family?

I do not presume anything about family make-up. The principles can apply in virtually all family settings. However, I recognize that many types of family situations make discipline more of a challenge. Regardless, I have seen many non-traditional family settings (particularly single parent situations) where discipline is dealt with in a model fashion.

The information in this book is intended to be used with children who are between the ages of 4 and 12. With some modification, you can use some ideas with teenagers and others with 1 to 3 year olds. However, teens and toddlers each have their own special set of concerns, not addressed on these pages.

Effective discipline approaches and strategies can be applied to a wide range of problems, from minor ones, (like forgetting to do a chore or whining), to major ones, (like aggression or destructiveness). The goal of effective discipline is to take an active role in molding and shaping your child's behavior in a positive direction. As it is, we have enough negative influences to compete with that can shape our child's behavior (such as the wrong crowd of kids, TV, and our child's own inclinations).

Children are not all the same!

Even though everyone agrees that children are all different, we need to be reminded of this. Some children are naturally compliant and others are naturally "strong-willed."

Nosy neighbors, family members, friends, and people at the grocery store overlook this fact. Isn't is annoying to get advice from someone who is raising naturally cooperative children? This type of person often fails to understand that some children are inclined to be more defiant than others! These parents sometimes assume that because your child misbehaves more than hers, you are doing something wrong and she is doing something right. Although this *could* be true, the difference may be due to the different temperaments between children. For children who are *not* naturally compliant, parents try the usual methods, but with minimal success. Out of desperation, parents then use ineffective approaches which may make matters worse (like "giving in" to avoid a hassle).

Children who are naturally defiant are very likely to cause parents to use poor parenting practices. However, poor parenting practices *rarely* turn compliant children into defiant children. This is because parents with compliant children naturally display good parenting practices. Many parents I consult with regarding a misbehaving child also have one who presents no behavior problems. If defiance was caused by poor parenting, then *all* the children in the family would be defiant. But this is usually not the case.

Take heart! You probably didn't create your child's misbehavior. However, it is entirely possible that you have accidentally slipped into ineffective approaches that either keep your child from making progress, or that make matters worse. The following chapters will provide you with ways of reversing this process and help you to get control of your child's behavior.

What Doesn't Work, and Why

Many types of discipline which parents use are ineffective. You may be using some of them. They include lecturing, anger, yelling, threatening, ignoring, and permissiveness.

Why lectures are ineffective

From my experience, I find that many parents rely too heavily on giving kids lengthy explanations about their behavior. Parents become disappointed when their children's behavior does not improve. Kids respond much better to action than to lectures. A child deserves an explanation — the first time — and maybe even the second. After that, parents must take some kind of action to see that the child will act properly.

Parents often expect too much when they "have a talk with" their children. Sometimes this changes behavior, but the results usually don't last long. Let's put the issue in perspective. Let's say that you have a tendency to get to work late. Your boss lectures you about the importance of getting to work on time. For most people, this would not result in a long term change. But what if your boss said that your pay will be docked based upon arriving late? That would change your arrival habits quickly! For adults, actions speak louder than words — should we expect it to be different with children? If one explanation doesn't work, other explanations probably won't work either.

Why anger and hostility are ineffective

Parents often respond to misbehavior with anger and hostility. This type of response usually does not help. The anger is often directed at the *child* and does not address the *behavior*. Thus, parents can harm the child's self-esteem without helping the problem. Besides, we teach our children to respond angrily when they are frustrated. When children are disciplined by an angry parent, they associate their punishment with the parent's anger, not with their misbehavior. They think they are in trouble because of mom's or dad's mood, not because of what they did. Thus, they learn nothing.

Why yelling is ineffective

Yelling doesn't work well because kids get used to being yelled at. We think that if we say something *often* enough and *loud* enough, it will eventually sink in. The opposite is usually true! When we yell and nag, our kids learn to tune us out.

Why threats are ineffective

Often, in desperation, we make threats we do not intend to carry out. Our kids learn to see through this. When we make threats, children usually know we are bluffing. One mother heard that her second grade son was caught sticking up his middle finger at school. I heard her tell him, "If you do this again, I'll take you to the doctor's to have it cut off." The boy clearly knew that this would never happen.

When parents are out with their children, they often say, "If you don't behave, we're going home." Although this would be a reasonable consequence for misbehavior, parents are bluffing. Kids quickly learn what we will do and will not do. Threats are not an effective way to change behavior.

Why ignoring and permissiveness are ineffective

There are some situations where ignoring can be helpful in reducing misbehavior (see Chapter 5). However, under most circumstances, ignoring misbehavior actually makes it worse. Ignoring allows the child the opportunity to misbehave and teaches him that we are not concerned about his misbehavior.

Permissiveness works the same way. If we let our children do whatever they want, they can develop serious behavior problems as they grow up. Parents who are too permissive do not allow their children to learn limits and responsibility — two things they will need to become well adjusted adults.

Why counseling is ineffective for behavior change

Parents and school personnel often assume that misbehaving children ought to receive counseling. But counseling is rarely effective at changing misbehavior. Counseling can help children with various problems (anxieties, social stressors, grief, fears, and many other concerns), but usually does not change misbehavior. Children lack the mental maturity required to translate counseling insights into changed habits or behavior.

Effective Discipline

The best way to change a child's behavior is by changing the way parents, teachers, and other adults respond to that child. That is the basic premise of this book. *You* can improve your child's behavior. You can help your child reduce his or her[1] misbehavior, and help increase good behavior. As the parent, *you* are the one who needs to take the initiative to change your child's behavior. On the following pages you will learn the most important principles for managing misbehavior. Keep reading! The next step is up to you.

---

[1]Throughout this book I alternate the masculine and feminine pronouns.

Chapter 2

The Effective Discipline Approach

In this chapter, you will learn:
◊ How to effectively communicate your expectations to your child.
◊ How to effectively follow through with action when your child misbehaves.

In this chapter you will learn the two most basic steps of effective discipline. The information and ideas described in Chapters 3, 4, and 5 are the resources you will use to carry out this basic approach.

Good discipline involves two parts. The first part is teaching a child how to behave properly. The second part is giving the child a reason to behave properly. This second part refers to developing a better and better relationship with your child. Although this book primarily covers the first part of discipline (teaching the child to behave), some helpful information about self-esteem and relationship building is contained in Chapter 8 (and to a limited extent in Chapter 4).

Research by psychologists on family patterns has indicated that the most psychologically healthy pattern is the one where parents balance love and firmness. Whenever discipline simply becomes getting children to behave, parents become dictators, and children become resistent subjects. On the other hand, if parents do not provide any limits, chaos results. But when love and firmness are in balance, discipline becomes a matter of leading and guiding. This type of family atmosphere promotes growth and cooperation.

The Two-Step Effective Discipline Approach

Effective discipline can be accomplished by two steps. Although these steps are simple, they are not easy. They may be simple to understand, but they are not always easy to put into practice. The two steps to effective discipline are as follows:

1. *Clearly state your expectations.*
2. *Follow through with action.*

At first, this may seem too simple to be helpful. But a little bit of explanation will show that these steps are the framework for using a wide variety of useful discipline strategies.

Step 1: *Clearly state your expectations*

Children do not automatically grow up knowing how they should act. We have to tell them. Yet this first step in effective discipline is the point where many attempts at discipline fail. When expectations are unclear or when expectations frequently change, children are not sure what to do. Therefore, their only option is to do what they think they should do (i.e., they "do what they darn well please!").

Be Specific. Sometimes we parents think we are being very direct and clear, yet we do not realize how unclear and non-specific our words actually are. Here are some typical kinds of things we say to our children:

Behave yourselves!	Act your age	Be good
Grow up, will ya?	Please cooperate	Be nice
Stop making me mad	Quit acting stupid	

None of these statements help a child understand what you expect from him. For example, before leaving the house a mother tells her son, "You behave when we're at Grandma's." This does not tell him much. It only tells him that his mom will have her eye on him while they are at Grandma's.

Effective discipline must start with clearly understood expectations. In the case of the trip to Grandma's house, it would make more sense for the mother to select between one and three misbehaviors that her child is likely to do while at

Grandma's house. Then she would explain her expectations about those behaviors. This way, the lines are clearly drawn as to what the mother wants. (If too many behaviors are discussed ahead of time, the child will be more likely to forget or tune mom out.) While at Grandma's, other behaviors may occur that she did not discuss ahead of time. In this case, she will have to make her expectations clear as each situation arises.

It is important for parents to learn to think *specifically* about what they want from their children. For example, two children are fighting over a toy:

Non-specific: "Billy, be nice to your brother."
Specific: "Billy, please let your brother have a turn."

The first statement may leave the child unsure of what you want. The second statement leaves no room for doubt.

Communicate nonverbally. An important part of communication is non-verbal. You may want to stand face to face when you speak. Make sure she is looking at you.[1] This will communicate your message more clearly than by yelling your expectation from the next room. However, you should never point your finger in her face or do anything that she might think is humiliating. This might make her resentful and more uncooperative.

Be positive. Parents who make it a habit of speaking in a positive fashion will promote cooperation. It is easy to slip into stating expectations negatively. But even negative things can be stated positively. For example, consider the following:

Negative: Jason, quit being a jerk. You keep your grimy little hands off his project. If you touch it one more time, you'll be in your room so fast your head will spin.

Positive: Jason, you must not touch your brother's project. He has worked very hard on it. If you touch it again, you'll have to stay in your room until dinner.

The negative approach sends many messages that attack the child as a person but do not help change behavior. The

---

[1]This refers to making sure your child is paying attention to your instructions. When reprimanding a child, I'm not sure it's a good idea to make her look at you.

positive approach conveys your expectation in a way that will preserve self-esteem and increase the chances for cooperation. Parents must learn to avoid speaking out of their frustration and be careful with their words. Likewise, name calling ("what a jerk," "you're a brat") or labeling children with negative characteristics ("you're just lazy," "that's so stupid") never promotes better behavior, cooperation, or self-esteem. These negative messages only discourage children and make them *less* likely to cooperate.

Be brief. I saw a sign at a laundromat which said "The more you say, the less people will remember." This is true of parents and their children. Long, drawn out explanations do not help. Brief, clear directions do.

Ask for feedback. Under many circumstances, you may want to ask your child if he understands what is expected. Having him explain the expectations back to you will let you know if he understands or not. It allows you the opportunity to correct any misunderstandings, right from the start.

Present consequences as choices. When you communicate your expectations, often there are consequences attached. For example, you might say "You won't be able to go outside until you finish cleaning your room." In such cases, it may be helpful to present the consequence as the child's choice. Your child "chooses" to stay inside by not finishing her room. She has control over whether or not she goes outside by either cleaning her room or not. Therefore, you are not making her stay inside, she is keeping herself inside when she does not clean her room. By stating consequences as a choice, you are putting the responsibility on your child. You are teaching her that she is accountable for her own decisions.

Focus on the behavior, not the child. When stating expectations, it is important to focus on the behavior, and not make statements about the child. For example, to say, "you must not leave any clothing on the floor" focuses on the behavior while "look at these clothes all over, you're such a slob" is a personal insult. By making a global statement about the child as a person ("you're lazy," "you're such a brat," etc.), you do nothing to help the situation. You only discourage the child by such name calling. When you focus on the behavior, you take a constructive approach to the situation.

Do not let arguing hinder your communication. Some of you already know that when you state your expectations, your child is going to argue about it. Do not let this happen because it will hinder your ability to communicate your expectations. You can virtually eliminate arguing by using one of three techniques described in Chapters 5 and 9.

Let them know when you like something! It is easy for parents to get into the pattern of warning or reprimanding their children about misbehavior, yet not saying anything positive about their good behavior. This is very unfortunate. We must tell our children when they behave in a way that we like. Kids need that kind of encouragement to behave better. Here is a story that illustrates this: There was a 10 year old boy who had never spoken from birth. He had no medical reason for being mute, so he was a mystery. One day his mother put his supper in front of him and he said "Hey, this food is burnt!" His parents were shocked to hear him say his first words. They asked him, "after all these years, why didn't you ever say anything?" He responded, "Because everything has been fine until now." In the same way, we parents become verbal when our children misbehave, but remain "mute" when they behave acceptably. *We must routinely praise and encourage our children when they display good behavior* (see Chapter 4).

Step Two: Follow through with Action

The first step to effective discipline is to clearly state your expectations. In order to be clear, you need to be specific. Both you and the child should be 100% clear about what is expected and what is not. But even when your child knows what you want, he will still misbehave in many cases. In those situations, you move to the second step: Follow through with action.

The goal of following through with action is to help establish a link between a behavior and a consequence. If the behavior is good, you want to reinforce and encourage it. If the child associates the good behavior with positive outcomes, he will be more likely to show good behavior in the future. If misbehavior is followed by unpleasant consequences, your child will learn that it is not worth misbehaving. If you do not follow through with action (or you follow through inconsistently), you miss a valuable opportunity to shape your child's behavior in a positive direction.

Parents often fail at discipline because they seem to be trying to win a popularity contest with their kids. We are quick to let our children off the hook, give extra chances, compromise, or in some other way not follow through with action. From this, our children learn that they can misbehave with no negative consequence, so there is no reason to stop misbehaving. When a parent decides to consistently follow through with action, it sends the message that misbehavior will not be tolerated.

You will begin to see positive changes in your child's behavior when you begin to consistently follow through with action. If you have been taking action yet do not see the positive change you want, keep reading. In the next chapter, you will learn about what makes one action effective and another ineffective. In the four chapters after that, you will learn a wide variety of effective techniques to use when you decide to take action. Below are several things to keep in mind when you follow through with action.

Do not back down. In any relationship, including the parent-child relationship, there is give and take, accommodation and compromise. This is okay. However, when it comes to discipline, it is important that you do not back down once you have decided to follow through with action. If you back down, you send the message to your child that she can get her way by pleading and pestering. This will teach her to pester you more and more when you punish her. In the long run, you will become more frustrated because you let her undermine your efforts at discipline. For example, if you tell your child she has to stay inside the rest of the evening because of misbehavior, you must see to it that she stays inside all evening, regardless of how much she pleads with you. You simply state that she will have another opportunity tomorrow, and leave it at that. If she persists in arguing, you can use one the the techniques for ending arguments described in Chapters 5 and 9.

Avoid giving extra chances. Here is a common mistake parents make with discipline. It is similar to what was described above. When children misbehave and are going to be punished, they often quickly become remorseful to avoid the punishment. They will plead for one more chance, and parents often give in. But it would be better for the parent to follow through with some small but meaningful consequence than to allow any more chances. The child will have a whole new set of chances after they have experienced a consequence. This may seem rather cold and heartless, but the fact is that *children usually do not learn to stop misbehaving by getting extra chances.* When you give extra chances, they learn how to get you to back down! The exception to this is when your child has been very cooperative and slips up once on something you warned him about. In virtually all other circumstances, you should follow through with action every time the child misbehaves, even if he asks for "one more chance." To make it easier to follow through, it is better to set up a small punishment that you would not hesitate to use. This is discussed more fully in the next chapter under the "Less is More Principle."

Nip misbehavior in the bud. One major advantage of taking action immediately is that it avoids a lot of frustration. Parents often do not take action when a child misbehaves because they are not mad enough at the child yet. They let the child get by with just a reprimand or warning, but do not take action until the child misbehaves several times. For example:

> Dad is watching TV and Chris keeps pestering his sister. Dad keeps telling him to stop, but each time Chris is back at it within minutes. Finally, Dad gets frustrated (because he's not able to watch TV without interruptions) and blows his stack and sends his son to his room for the night.

If, on the other hand, the father decided to nip the problem in the bud, the scene would have been more like this:

Dad is watching TV and Chris pesters his sister once. Dad turns away from the TV and immediately deals with Chris. He has Chris sit at the kitchen table for five minutes (where he cannot amuse himself with anything). After the five minutes, he goes back to play, but does not bother his sister. He has learned over time that his father gives him a consequence *every time* he misbehaves.

In this second scenario, the dad avoided much hassle and aggravation by taking action early in the situation. He nipped the problem in the bud by not allowing the situation to escalate as it did in the first scenario.

You may object and say "I can't respond every time my child misbehaves, that would take all of my time." The father in the first scenario would have felt the same way. But most of that misbehavior would not have occurred if he nipped it in the bud. It only occurred because he allowed it to occur by inaction (and warnings are a form of inaction). However, when parents nip misbehavior in the bud, they decrease the chance it will happen again.

If you begin to use this "bud nipping" principle, you may find that it takes several times for your child to get the message. That is because he will not be accustomed to you responding every time he misbehaves. He still thinks that you are not going to respond every time, so he continues to misbehave. After you have consistently taken action he will finally learn that you will respond every time. Only then will he decide to stop the misbehavior. I cannot emphasize enough how important it is to nip misbehavior in the bud instead of letting several incidences go by before taking action. You will begin to see great results when you use this principle.

Avoid the warning trap. When a child is warned again and again about the same or similar misbehavior, he learns that he can continue to misbehave because it is not likely that anything is going to be done about it. Do you ever catch yourself saying "how many times do I have to tell you?" If you do, then you have probably fallen into the warning trap. The solution is simple. Once a child has been warned, take action every time the child misbehaves that way — with no further warnings.

You will be amazed at how soon the behavior improves.

Consider the following example: John never seems to respond on the first call when he is told to pick up his toys, come to dinner, or get ready for bed. His mother scolds, bribes, and threatens. Mom cannot understand the problem.

John has learned his mother's patterns. He knows that the first time she says "John, pick your toys," she really does not mean business. What she means is "John, I am giving you the first of a series of requests to pick up your toys. You might as well continue to play for a while longer, because I'm not going to do anything about it yet." John is no dummy. He knows from experience when mom means business, and when she does not. He knows that he can avoid doing what he doesn't want to by not responding to her warnings and requests. Only when mom has finally blown her stack (after the fifth or sixth warning) will he have to do what he was told. Her pattern of giving many warnings has "trained" him to *not* respond on the first (or second) call.

Not getting in the last word. Many parents try to get in the last word when they discipline. At the same time, the child tries to get in the last word. This lengthens the confrontation. Each side is trying to stay "one up" on the other. As a parent, your most important task of discipline is to make sure you get in the *last action*. It is not necessary to get in the last word, as long as you get in the last action. If you stop trying to get in the last word, confrontations will die down sooner.

Your child does not "win" the confrontation when he gets in the last word. If you take action, that action will be the final say in the matter. For example, Kevin is disciplined and begins to argue with his father about it, but his dad does not give in. In the course of the discussion, Kevin gets in the last word ("you're so mean, you never let me do anything"). His dad chooses not to respond to it. Kevin says it again, but his dad does not respond, so the situation begins to cool down. Because dad sticks to the punishment, the boy learns that even when he tries to "win" with the last word, he still experiences the consequences. If you are working on your child's "mouthiness" you will not want to allow him to get in the last word.[2] However, most of the time, you need to rise above such verbal confrontations and simply see to it that the "final word" is the consequence, not the child's verbal attacks.

Avoid the "I don't care" syndrome. Often when a parent attempts to use discipline, the child simply says "I don't care." This is usually the case when a parent withdraws a privilege or sends the child to her room. When a child says this, she usually *does* care, but she is trying to do one of two things. First, she may be trying to get the parent to back down or compromise on the consequence, because the parent may think the punishment is not going to help. Second, which is more likely, she is simply trying to "save face," and act as if the punishment does not bother her. If your child says "I don't care" when you provide a consequence, she is probably trying to manipulate you.

When children use the "I don't care" tactic, parents often feel frustrated and think their efforts don't work. By knowing that your child is really trying to manipulate you, you will see that the solution is simple. When you assign a consequence and your child says "I don't care," *don't back down.* Confidently follow through with the consequence. Ignore "I don't care" statements and continue to use this approach in the future. If the approach does not work after weeks of consistent use, then maybe the child really did not care. This is unlikely. If you are consistent, the child will usually begin to avoid the misbehavior that results in the consequence. This will happen even if she never admits that she really did care about the punishment.

Action speaks louder than words. The bottom line is that actions teach children to improve behavior, and words (by themselves) do not. When you take action quickly and consistently, you teach your child that there is a consequence to misbehavior. He will learn to avoid consequences by avoiding misbehavior. Our goal as parents is for our children to learn to "internalize" good behavior (i. e., learn right from wrong). But this does not happen automatically. Because of their developmental level, children are not yet capable of behaving based

---

[2]For dealing with mouthiness, see Chapter 9.

upon some higher moral standard or ideal. As children grow older, this internalizing is bound to occur. It seems reasonable to assume that the best environment for this growth to occur is a home with a healthy balance of love and firm limits, where children feel comfortable communicating with their parents.

When you provide limits, carried out in a loving fashion, your child will learn to recognize that he has much freedom within those limits. At my house, we live by a busy road. We have a fence around our back yard. Our young children have learned that they are not to leave the yard without adult supervision because of the obvious dangers. They comfortably play within the limits of the yard. There is a sand box, a swing set, toys, and open space. They have much freedom to have fun, to play, and run. Yet they have definite limits indicated by a chain-link fence. Even though they are aware of the limits, they have learned to be happy within them. In the same way, your children can comfortably learn to live within the limits you set in your home. However, they may frequently challenge those limits, especially if they are not consistently maintained.

The fence in my backyard is very consistent. It never moves, yields, or compromises. Our kids have never complained about the fence. Yet if some days the fence was in closer and some days it was out farther, you can bet they would plead with me to keep moving it out farther and farther. Of course it never changes, so they never think to challenge the limits the fence provides. In the same way, when parents do not maintain consistent limits, our children challenge us to see where the limits are for that particular day. When you provide firm, consistent limits, you are providing your child with a secure environment where he or she understands what is expected from him, and what he can expect from you. You can allow much freedom to give your child the opportunity to learn and grow, while maintaining firm, consistent limits.

SUMMARY

The basic formula for successful discipline is very simple to learn and remember, even if it may be difficult carry out. It involves two basic steps:

1) *Clearly state your expectations.* It is very important that your child understands what you want in advance. There must be no room for uncertainty about your expectations. State your expectations in a clear, specific, brief, and positive way.

2) *Follow through with action.* When your child misbehaves, take action to see that he does what you expect. This action must be immediate and consistent if he is going to learn. Firm limits must be maintained, but limits must be balanced with love and encouragement. If your child behaves the way you want him to, let him know you appreciate it. Taking action is not limited to providing consequences for misbehavior. Taking action also involves reinforcing good behavior.

By taking action and using consequences with misbehavior, you are simply trying to lead and guide your child, not harass them or turn them into little robots. As an adult, you know that certain behavior will ultimately make your child (and others in the family) unhappy as he grows up, so you want to discourage such behavior. Also, you want to actively encourage positive behavior. You must take charge of guiding your child's behavior. You do not want to leave that important job to your child's own short-term self interest, his peers, TV, or a popular culture which often encourages undesirable behavior. When you lead and guide, you are taking an active role in your child's behavioral, emotional, social, and moral development.

Now that you know the basics of effective discipline, you are ready to explore a variety of ways, both positive and corrective, to promote good behavior. In the following three chapters, you will learn many practical aspects of taking action. The next step is up to you. You can help make a positive change in your child. Taking an active role in your child's development can produce many benefits in the years to come.

Chapter 3

Keys to Improving Behavior

In this chapter you will learn:
- ◊ What makes discipline effective and why discipline is often ineffective.
- ◊ Several keys to help your children understand the consequences of their behavior.
- ◊ Several keys to help you follow through when using discipline.

Wouldn't it be nice if you had a brand new Mercedes-Benz and a new Corvette sitting in your driveway? But what if you had no keys to operate them? They would not be very useful. The same is true for discipline strategies. The most clever strategy is not going to be helpful if you do not have the keys to operate it. In this chapter, some of the most important "keys" to effective discipline are presented.

I have found that parents are always looking for better strategies for discipline, but it is these "keys to improving behavior" that they need most. Many good interventions have failed because one or more of the keys were not used. Parents then assume that the discipline strategy is ineffective or there is something wrong with their child. I have consulted with many parents who successfully improved their child's behavior using their old strategies which they thought didn't work! They became successful because they applied those old strategies in an effective manner using the keys presented below.

It was intentional that the chapter on keys to improving

behavior was placed before the two chapters on techniques for improving behavior. Parents often search for the perfect strategy, idea, or technique not realizing that the *proper use* of a strategy is usually the most important part of the process. So please do not feel tempted to skip ahead to the "bag of tricks" in the following two chapters. The information in this chapter deserves careful reading and rereading in order to make your efforts more effective.

Why the "Keys" Work

Did you ever consider the fact that children do not disobey the laws of gravity? Of course many kids like to do daring stunts, but no child thinks he can walk out a window expecting to walk through the air. Why is there such universal obedience to the laws of gravity? Awareness of gravity is not an instinct in human babies — infants have to learn not to mess with mother nature. If the limits of gravity have to be learned, why do children learn them so well yet learn discipline so poorly? What makes gravity such a good teacher?

The reason gravity is such a good teacher is that from early on, babies and children learn that there are consequences to disobeying gravity. Unlike the consequences we parents provide, the consequences of disobeying gravity are consistent, immediate, and generalized.

Consistent. The effects of gravity occur *every* time someone tries to "disobey" them. There is never a time when an attempt to defy gravity actually succeeds. No warnings and no second chances are involved. Children learn early that they will never walk in the air or float down the stairs if they fall. Gravity's consequences are 100% consistent.

Immediate. The consequences of gravity are immediate. Not only do they happen every time, they happen instantly. Therefore, a child quickly learns the connection between behavior (falling from the end table) and the consequence (the pain of landing on the floor).

Generalized. The consequences of disobeying gravity happen no matter where or when they occur. They happen in the home, out in public, and they happen regardless of the child's or parent's mood.

It is unreasonable to suggest that any parent can be 1) 100% consistent, 2) always provide immediate consequences, and 3) be able to provide the same level of effectiveness no matter when or where a misbehavior occurs. This would be impossible. But, the more consistent, immediate, and generalized we are in our discipline, the more effective it will be.

The "keys to improving behavior" described below are ways to help your child learn there is a connection between behavior and consequence. This is your goal. The connection between behavior and consequences can be strengthened or weakened depending on how well these keys are used. Your child must learn there are limits to behavior in the social world. Disregarding limits results in undesirable consequences. You want him to understand limits in order to carefully and lovingly shape his behavior to be appropriate and acceptable. The goal is to prepare children for social, behavioral, and moral competency as they mature toward adulthood. As your child grows, your words and good example, along with the direction your provide through rewards and consequences, will help him to "internalize" good behavior.

I. Keys that Help Children Make the Connection Between Behavior and Consequence

1. Consistency

Before any attempts to change a child's behavior will be successful, the parent must be consistent with that child. In 95 out of 100 situations where a child has a behavior problem, careful assessment will reveal that some adult (a parent or teacher) is being inconsistent in their discipline. This does not mean that the parent or teacher created the problem, only that inconsistency can facilitate or worsen the problem. No parent is perfect, and no one is absolutely consistent. *But the major difference between parents who discipline effectively and those who do not is their level of consistency.*

Virtually all parents agree that consistency is important. However, we are often unaware of hidden forms of inconsistency in day to day dealings with our children. Here are a few kinds of inconsistency that commonly occur:

1. *Idle threats.* A child quickly learns which threats are genuine and which ones are not. If parents rely on idle threats, they teach their child that there will be no real consequence for misbehavior. The inconsistency is between the parent's threats and actions (i.e., no follow through).

2. *Multiple warnings.* When a child is warned over and over, he learns that he can continue to misbehave because the chances are very slim that any action will be taken. Do you ever catch yourself asking "How many times do I have to tell you . . . ?" If you do, then you have fallen into the *warning trap*, described in the last chapter. The solution to this problem is simple. Once your child has been warned about the consequences of a behavior, take action *every time* he misbehaves that way — with no further warnings. You may need to give younger children (ages 4 to 6) one warning per day for each misbehavior, then take action. For older children, today's warning should cover the next week. If you remove the warnings, you will be amazed at how soon the behavior decreases.

3. *Extra chances.* Often when children are caught misbehaving, they quickly apologize, or promise to not do it any more. Usually, they do this in order to avoid consequences. But giving children "extra chances" after a misbehavior teaches them they can sweet talk their way out of trouble. They then have no reason to stop misbehaving in the future. Remember, children will always get plenty of chances to display proper behavior *after* the consequence. Ordinarily, there is no benefit to giving an extra chance (unless, of course, it was the first incidence of this particular misbehavior and your child did not understand that it was wrong).

4. *Negotiating with terrorists.* Giving in to whining and nagging is a common form of inconsistency. Parents often take a stand on something, but after the child whines and pesters long enough, the parent gives in. Parents give in so they can escape the child's badgering. The child learns that he can get his way by annoying the parent. Techniques to avoid arguing and whining are discussed later in this book.

5. *Inconsistent consequences & limits.* Only providing a consequence some of the time is a form of inconsistency. It teaches a child that there will be a good chance he will not be held accountable for the misbehavior. The child then decides it is worth the risk to misbehave.[1] With each misbehavior that goes unpunished, the child feels more and more confident about misbehaving. Often, children are like little gamblers. They take calculated risks based upon how they think their parents will respond. *If they know that they only get punished some of the time, they misbehave.*

Parents often punish based upon mood. If you have guidelines you expect your children to follow, do not bend them because you are in a "laid-back" mood, or a lazy mood (i.e., you do not feel like getting out of your chair to take action). Also, if your rules change from one day to the next, your child will have a hard time learning limits. Often rules are based upon the parent's tolerance of a behavior at the moment. This usually results in no progress in the child's behavior. You must decide on expectations and stick with those expectations regardless of your mood or tolerance level at the moment.

There are many ways we can have a lapse of consistency. Each lapse of consistency weakens the connection between behavior and consequence. This increases the chance of future misbehavior. It cannot be stressed enough that parents will not

---

[1]When I say that "a child learns to . . ." or "the child decides . . ." it must be understood that I am saying this from an adult perspective. Most of these "decisions" are without much deliberate, conscious thought by children.

see improvement if they are not consistent with their children. Even though no one can ever be 100% consistent, we can all improve our level of consistency. *Parents should make consistency the number one priority in disciplining their child.*

2. *Timing*

In order for your son or daughter to make the connection between a behavior and its consequence, the action you take should occur as soon as possible following the behavior. Punishing a child for something she did two hours ago usually does not work. Praising a child at night for something she did that morning probably will not improve behavior. When a child misbehaves, it will be necessary to apply a negative consequence right when she misbehaves. When a child does something good, she should be told right away. When a child experiences an immediate consequence for her behavior, she can more easily make the connection between the behavior and the consequence. Then her behavior will begin to improve.

There is another issue about timing. If you decide to use an incentive with your child, do not set it up a long time in advance. For example, don't say, "If you keep your room clean all week, I'll let you rent a video on Friday." For most kids, this is too long of a time to keep an incentive in mind to motivate them. The same goes for consequences. If you warn your child that he will not go roller skating next week if he misbehaves today, you are setting a consequence too far in the future.[2]

I hear parents describe big, long-term rewards or punishment they have used with their child. I've heard, "He knows that if his grades improve this marking period, he'll get a new bike" or "I keep telling him that if he keeps up his back-talk, I'll yank his Nintendo someday." Parents are then disappointed when no improvement occurs. Incentives and consequences must be minute to minute, hour to hour, or day to day. *Setting a goal too far in the future is an ineffective way to change behavior.*

[2]The only way to make use of an incentive in the future is by using a token system of reinforcement described in Chapter 4.

There is an age consideration with timing. Older children (pre-teens) can work better with longer time periods. Younger children (4 to 7) are more impulsive and do not understand time as well. But even pre-teens do better with short-term goals and incentives. Remember, the closer the reward or consequence is to the behavior, the more likely the child will learn and remember the connection between their behavior and the reward or consequence.

3. Proximity

Often it is important to use your physical presence to effectively influence behavior. This is called *proximity*. For example, yelling from the other room to tell your child to pick up his toys before dinner probably won't work. But if you walk over and stand close to your child, look him in the eye, and calmly but firmly make your request, he is more likely to do what you say. When you use your physical presence in this way, you are communicating that you mean business.

You must be willing to routinely get up from what you are doing and head in the direction of your child when it becomes clear that your words are not being followed. If this is done consistently, your child will learn that mom or dad will be following through with action *every time.* Eventually, he will do what you say most of the time based on your words alone. You must not feel "put out" when you have to get up and cross the room to see to it that your child complies. Rather, you should see it as a "training session" that teaches him that you will not tolerate misbehavior. The more consistently you do this, the sooner he will begin to do what you ask.

Physical persuasion. Another effective way to gain compliance with a resistent child is *physical persuasion*. This means that you may need to "escort" your child to his room, to the tub, or away from an activity when he is being resistent. Unfortunately, when children are resistant, parents often scream, hit, or walk away saying "I don't know what to do with you!" It would make more sense to simply take the action necessary to get the child to do what is expected.

In one situation, a mother would not send her 10 year old son to his room because whenever she tried, he resisted strongly. Finally she decided to use "physical persuasion." The next time she told him to go upstairs to his room, she escorted him there. It was exhausting for her because he kicked and yelled, swung his arms about, and firmly grabbed onto the stair railing. She had to pry his hands free from the railing and continue on her way. The next time she told him to go to his room, he resisted in the same way, except he did not clutch the stair railing. The next time after that, he refused to go to his room, but did not fight her as she dragged him there. Finally, he began to go to his room on his own when told. By her use of physical persuasion, he learned that mom was serious, and it was not worth the struggle for him because he saw no chance of succeeding.

In many cases, physical persuasion may be needed for the resistent child, although extreme caution must be taken. Children should not be pulled by an arm, grabbed by the hair or neck, etc. Safety must be a priority when using physical persuasion. The purpose is to show the child that he will comply no matter what, and there is no room for risk of injury. Also, screaming at the child in these situations only agitates the child even more, while calm, reassuring, yet firm words may help the child to settle down.

4. The 24 Hour Rule and the Time Block Approach

Another key to effective discipline is to keep consequences within a 24 hour period or less. If a child has TV withdrawn for three nights, parents may have to argue the issue for all three nights. What if the child has a great day during one of the three days of his punishment? Should the parent give in and allow him to watch? No, parents must stick with their word. But by using long punishments, parents create these awkward situations. Parents end up punishing themselves — they have to deal with the child's complaining, pleading, and resentment.

Another drawback to long, drawn out punishments or restrictions is that it decreases the parents ability to provide additional consequences. Let's say a child is restricted from going outside after school to play for three days. What do you do if the child acts up on day two? Usually parents try to find something else to take away. I have consulted with parents that have said, "We don't understand, our child isn't getting the message. Right now he has no TV, no Nintendo, and no playing outside for two weeks." This is an ineffective way to administer consequences. The time span is too long for the child to make the proper connections, parents have to struggle extra hard to follow through for two full weeks, and the child's resentment can build as time goes by. Also, if a child has several things removed for a few days or more, he might think he can misbehave because he no longer has anything to lose. Parents have nothing left to "hold over his head" when he misbehaves during this time. In addition, this approach often is ineffective because parents are so burdened by trying to enforce a lengthy punishment that they give in, teaching their children that they are not going to follow through.

A more effective approach is to keep the withdrawal of a privilege within a 24 hour period. *Effectiveness does not increase by giving longer punishments.* Every day, a child should be given a fresh start to demonstrate acceptable behavior. Another way to apply this principle is to think in terms of *time blocks.* One time block could run from the time the child comes home from school until dinner. Another is between dinner and bedtime. On weekends, meals can provide dividing lines for time blocks. In many cases, parents could restrict their punishments to one time block instead of a whole day. How long to withdraw a privilege depends upon several things, including how frequently the child displays the specific misbehavior you are trying to correct. If the misbehavior occurs frequently, punishment for one time block makes sense. This way the child has 2-3 opportunities in a single day to learn that his parents are serious about dealing with the misbehavior. If the behavior is more serious in nature, restrictions for the remainder of the day might be more appropriate.

When you use the 24 hour or *time block* approaches, your child will have more fresh starts, without actually giving him any "extra chances." After the consequence, you "forgive and forget" and allow your child more opportunities to learn the consequences of misbehavior. If you think this is too "light" of a punishment, see the section below called "Less is more."

5. *Control Your Emotions*

Discipline is most effective when it is administered in a calm, controlled fashion. This may seem unrealistic, but it is not. It is necessary to keep your emotions in control for several reasons. First, if you yell and scream, *your child will associate the consequence with your mood rather than with his behavior.* Kids can think they are being punished because mom or dad is in a bad mood instead of understanding that they are receiving a consequence for misbehavior.

Another reason for calm discipline is that many children like to see that they have the power to upset their parents. If discipline is done in a calm way, you remove that reward for misbehavior.

A third reason for calm discipline is that if a parent is angry, he or she is more likely to use an inappropriate form of discipline that will not be effective. For example, when angry, a parent might give an overly severe punishment ("That's it, you're grounded for a week!"). In these cases, the severity of the punishment resulted from the parent's desire to vent frustration, not from careful discipline.

Parents often rely too heavily on yelling, screaming, and pleading with their children because it seems to work for the moment. This results in not using a more effective approach that is more likely to have a lasting effect. If you can discipline calmly, you can rely on more effective approaches, and your kids will learn more quickly. *Actions speak louder than words —*

even loud words!

A fourth reason to keep from using anger when you discipline is that it teaches your children to behave with anger and hostility. Your example teaches them to lash out when they get frustrated. This is not a good social skill to teach! Your children will be less likely to lash out as much when they do not have an angry parent to "learn" from. Also, if you discipline your children without anger, your children will be less likely to use anger to discipline when they grow up and become parents.

A final reason is that if you allow yourself to get upset, your ability to think clearly and make proper decisions is affected in such angry situations. You increase the likelihood that you will "fly off the handle" and harm your child emotionally or physically. Parental anger and hostility usually results in an attack upon a child's self-esteem and does not help the child behave better in the future. Also, when acting in anger, parents might take out their frustration on their children by physically abusing them. *Anger and hostility do not make discipline more effective, but they can make it less effective.*

6. Less is more

Here is the best kept secret in child discipline: *In most cases, smaller rewards or punishments work better than larger ones.* This is true because it is easier for parents to be consistent with smaller reinforcers and consequences than with larger ones. Smaller rewards and consequences involve less of a parent's time and effort. If a consequence or reward is large, a parent may be reluctant to use it, and no discipline occurs (except for ineffective warnings, threats, or yelling). As mentioned above, consistency is the most important key to improving behavior. Therefore, because small rewards and consequences can help parents with consistency, they boost effectiveness.

Some people reject this idea because they think such rewards and consequences are too small to be effective. But if consistently applied, small rewards and consequences can be very effective. Consider the following example. You are driving your car too fast, and a police officer stops you and gives you a $2 ticket. You are quite relieved, and try to keep from laughing. The next day, you are again stopped and the policeman again issues a $2 ticket. You are still surprised and amused, and wonder if this guy is serious. This continues *every time* you speed. Eventually, the tickets start to add up, not to mention the time and hassle of being stopped, and the cost and effort involved in sending in the tickets. Besides, you get to your destination late when you were in a hurry to begin with. Because of these consequences, and because you experience them *every* time you speed, you decide to drive within the limit. The *consistent application* of $2 speeding tickets would do more to stop your speeding habits than all of the warnings about a $75 ticket. Remember, it is the consistent use of a consequence, not the severity, that will improve behavior.

The same is the case with parents and children. A child who receives regular small punishments will be more likely to reduce his misbehavior than a child who receives frequent warnings and occasional large punishments. Also, children who are rarely reinforced, but occasionally get big incentives will not improve as much as a child who often receives small reinforcers. Remember, it is the *consistency, not the severity,* that makes a consequence or reinforcement effective.

Another reason why small incentives and punishers work better is that it gives more opportunities for learning. Parent #1 sent her child to his room for roughhousing after several warnings. The child spent the evening in his room reading books and playing with his toys. He eventually forgot why he was there. Parent #1 got the child out of the way for the evening, but there was little likelihood that any lessons were learned. Instead, the mother warned, yelled, and threatened until she finally got angry enough and followed through on the large punishment. The situation was escalating with each warning, so when the punishment was finally given, the child thought the consequence was a result of his mother's mood.

Parent #2 had her son sit by himself in a chair (away from TV, toys, or other amusements) for 5 minutes for roughhousing after one warning. When the time was up, his mother told him that she would not tolerate roughhousing. She said if he continued to misbehave in this way he would get another 5 minutes in the chair *with no further warnings*. It took 4 times in the chair that night, and her child got the message that his mom would follow through on her words *every* time. Now he listens to his mother when she tells him not to roughhouse, although he still occasionally tests her to see if she will follow through. Her discipline was successful because she consistently followed through with every instance of misbehavior. It was easy for her to follow through because the consequence was a small one, and she did not feel bad about using it. She did not even need to get angry. Also, she had several opportunities in one evening to demonstrate that she was serious and consistent, and her son had more opportunities to learn the lesson.

Nip misbehavior in the bud. There is a final reason why a small punisher would be more effective than a larger one. Because parents hesitate to use a big punishment on their children, they allow a situation to escalate before they act. With a small consequence, they would be more likely to nip the problem in the bud instead of letting it get out of hand. Parents can control their anger level by taking action early on in the situation, instead of letting things continue until the parent "hits the boiling point."

In summary, there are three important reasons why the *less is more* principle works. First, you are more likely to follow through with a smaller reward or punishment because it involves less time, energy, and guilt. When you are more consistent about giving a consequence, your child will get the clear message that you are not going to allow him to misbehave. Second, your child is more likely to make the connection between behavior and consequence because he is not going to associate his consequence with your mood. You do not let the situation escalate by giving many warnings and threats. Rather, you nip the misbehavior in the bud. Because you take action early in the situation — before you get upset — discipline is administered in a calm, controlled fashion. Finally, because the punishment in the above example was brief, it allowed that child more learning opportunities to discover his mom was serious about stopping the misbehavior. In the example of Parent #1, there were no such opportunities.

7. Make Changes One Step at a Time

Think of how confusing it can be when you start a new job and you have dozens of new things to remember. Children can feel the same way when their parents try to change too many things at the same time. Children can become very confused and frustrated if they suddenly have many new demands. This can also happen if mom and dad suddenly decide to take all those old demands seriously. You should select one or two behaviors to work on at a time (three behaviors at the most). After you see definite improvement you can work on additional behaviors.

Sometimes, when parents bring one area of behavior under control, others seem to fall into place almost automatically. This may be because the child learns mom and dad mean business. Suddenly, your words have more clout.

Another advantage to limiting the number of new demands is that *parents* are less confused. Extensive and complicated behavior plans are doomed from the start because there is too much for the parent to keep track of ("now what was I supposed to do when he does that?"). *The key is make few demands, communicate them clearly, and follow through on them consistently.*

II. Keys that Help Parents to
Make Changes and Follow Through

8. Behavior Often Gets Worse First!

When a parent tries to improve a child's behavior, the behavior often gets worse before it gets better. This happens because the child suddenly finds that he or she is no longer "in charge" and will try very hard to regain control.

It is important to know ahead of time that behavior might get worse before it gets better. This way you can mentally prepare yourself, and be more willing to keep up the new approach until your child improves. Parents often start a program of behavior change for their child but quit during this "worsening phase" because they think the plan is not working. The important thing to remember is that you are an adult, and they are children. You are mature enough that in the battle of wills, you can and must outlast them! If you give in during this worsening phase, *it will only make it harder the next time you try to make a change.* This is because your child will learn that if he puts up enough of a fuss, you will give in. You must learn to stick with it, or else you will not see the changes you want.

9. Immediate results may deceive

In some situations, parents may find their new plan gets immediate results. Because they see results, parents assume the problem is gone, so no more "remedy" is needed. Then, parents often go back to their old way of responding to their child. The parents get discouraged when the child also goes back to his old ways. A more reasonable approach would be to keep a rule or plan in place for a more extended period of time, until it is clear that the child has mastered it. In fact, many household rules stay in effect forever (e.g., no jumping on the couch, no playing ball indoors). Parents should be prepared to enforce rules long after the original problem seemed to have been resolved.

10. Gradual Improvement

Many parents expect too much too soon. An old proverb states "a journey of a thousand miles begins with a single step." A child's behavior will improve over time if parents carefully apply the principles of behavior improvement described in this book. However, improvement usually goes in stages. Remember, your child's current patterns of misbehavior may have taken weeks, months, or even years to develop. You cannot expect a change overnight. It may take weeks of effort using well planned and applied behavioral principles to see the results you want. It is amazing how many parents will try something once, twice, or three times and then discard the idea because "it didn't work." *There are some strategies and some situations where it may take 20 to 30 times before the child begins to show the desired change!* There are no quick and easy answers. Patience is important when you begin to take action.

Gradual improvement does not always mean steady progress. There are often ups and downs. It is during the down times that parents give up. However, patience and persistence pay off. Even as behavior improves, there are occasional relapses to which the parent must direct immediate attention. If they do not, the child can develop an old habit all over again.

An Illustration of Gradual Improvement

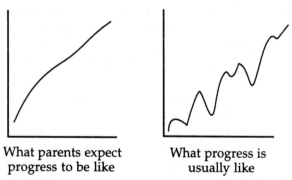

What parents expect   What progress is
progress to be like   usually like

11. *Honey tastes better than vinegar*

One very important key to improving behavior is to develop a better and better relationship with your child. Ben Franklin once said "you can catch more flies with a spoonful of honey than a barrelful of vinegar." If you are able to cultivate a positive relationship with your child, you will find yourself spending less time struggling over discipline issues.

You may say to yourself, "I have a great relationship with my child!" This may be true. A good relationship does not guarantee good behavior. However, the better the relationship, the more *likely* the child will be "on your side" when it comes to overall cooperation. One of the major issues is the amount of positive time you spend with your child. Studies suggest that parents often *think* they spend more personal time with their children than they actually do.

The buzz words we hear used these days are *quality* time vs. *quantity* time. *Quality time* is a term developed by very busy people who want to rid themselves of the guilt of being involved with too many other things besides their children. Many children do not know the difference between quality time and quantity time. Working parents can find quantity time to spend with their children if they really want to. Here are some questions that may help: How much time do you spend watching television? Most people watch more than they realize. Television is a diversion to pass the time and certainly can be cut to concentrate more time with your children. How much time do you spend on the telephone in the evening? How much job related work do you do at home? How many outside activities are you involved in during evening and on weekends (such as shopping, bowling, softball, being out with the guys, or girls, or any other interests)? The point is not to restrict yourself from doing anything. The challenge is to assess how much time is spent on things that should be a lower priority than your children.

Parents must create a balance between family and other activities. Kids can also become over-committed to outside interests. When this happens, parenting then becomes reduced to operating a shuttle service. Television also wastes many hours of the average child's day. Families must set priorities, and at the top of that list must be time and activities done together.

SUMMARY

When it comes to discipline, the important thing to remember is that *it is not necessarily what you do, but how you do it*. The above keys are divided into two categories; those that help the child understand the connection between behavior and consequence, and those that help the parent follow through on discipline. A child's behavior improves most when discipline is consistent, immediately follows the behavior, and with a parent standing next to him, dealing with him in a calm, controlled fashion. Discipline is best when given in small, consistent doses, and when only one or two behaviors are being worked on at a time. It will be important for parents to really learn the contents of this chapter and make this information part of their regular way of thinking through situations. Rereading the material will help to make it familiar enough to influence your thoughts and decisions about discipline as situations arise.

Chapter 4

How to Increase Good Behavior

In this chapter you will learn:
- ◊ Numerous strategies you can use to increase your child's good behavior.
- ◊ How to motivate good behavior by providing incentives for behavior.
- ◊ How to combine strategies to improve behavior.

There are many effective ways in which parents can increase and strengthen good behavior.[1] Most of these ways are not new. They have been carefully researched over the years and have been shown to be effective when used correctly. Some of the ideas presented here may be similar to what you have tried before. If you have tried one of the following suggestions and it did not work, it probably had something to do with the "keys to improving behavior" discussed in Chapter 3. Usually it is not the strategy that is ineffective, it is *how* the technique was used that resulted in little or no positive change. If you have skipped ahead in this book and have not carefully read the information in Chapter 3, please go back and read it. The material discussed there will determine whether any of the following ideas will work!

The goal of using incentives should always be to get children to "internalize" good behavior. This means you want your child to reach the point where he will behave well on his

---

[1]Techniques to reduce misbehavior will be covered in the next chapter.

own, without a lot of external reinforcement. Children can "internalize" behavior in one of two ways. First, a good behavior can develop into a habit, and therefore becomes the child's natural tendency. Second, a child can learn through reasoning that certain things should be done simply because they are the right thing to do. Younger children usually cannot behave for the second reason, but can for the first. In either case, progress takes time and effort.

Some parents refuse to use incentives. They think their child should "just do it." Yet adults are routinely motivated by external incentives. Why should we expect something different for kids? Imagine what would happen if your boss said to you, "we decided that we shouldn't have to pay you for this, you should 'just do it.'" I suspect you would get another job. In the real world, we are all motivated by external incentives. It is unreasonable to expect children to be internally motivated in their chores and good behavior. This is not to say kids should be "bribed" to behave. The point is that a healthy mix of the various types of reinforcers described in this chapter can help children develop more responsible behavior.

If consistently reinforced for responsible behavior, children grow up to develop good habits and learn the value of behaving responsibly. Then they will need fewer and fewer external incentives. Toilet training is a good example. Parents often provide treats or praise for successfully using the toilet while children are being trained. Yet what parent has to provide treats for their teenager for using the toilet? Obviously, there comes a point when a child can take responsibility for himself without the need for external rewards. But rewards and incentives help children "jump start" good habits and behavior.

The strategies described below have been grouped into two categories, positive reinforcement and avoidance reinforcement. *Positive reinforcement* increases good behavior because it can provide an incentive for good behavior. The child behaves because he is motivated by the incentive. *Avoidance* increases good behavior because the child feels he must behave a certain way to avoid something negative. For example, a child may finish making his bed because he cannot go outside until he does. This is reinforcement by avoidance. In order to avoid being stuck in the house, he has to make his bed. He is not making his bed because he *wants to*, he is doing it because he feels he *must* in order to keep from being stuck inside.

Parents can decide which strategies to use based upon 1) the type of behavior, 2) what they feel comfortable using, and 3) their knowledge of their child. Not every parent will feel comfortable with every approach described below.

Positive Reinforcement

Positive reinforcement provides a meaningful incentive for a child to behave properly. Often children see no benefit in behaving the way they should. An incentive may provide the motivation your child needs to behave the way you want. Remember, just because you want your child to behave a certain way does not mean he wants to behave that way. Providing positive reinforcement can teach him that there is a benefit to behaving the way you want him to. As mentioned, your goal is for him to internalize the good behavior, even if it takes a long time to reach that goal.

Keep in mind that positive reinforcement is designed to increase or encourage behavior. Generally, it has not been shown to be effective, by itself, in reducing misbehavior.[2] Teachers and parents often tell me, "Justin misbehaves despite the fact that I use positive reinforcement." They do not understand that Justin is deriving some benefit from the misbehavior or he would not be doing it. If he continues to receive a benefit for the misbehavior, he will continue to misbehave. Therefore, a behavior reduction strategy must be

---

[2]Positive reinforcement can be used *in combination* with other approaches to reduce misbehavior. This will be discussed in Chapter 5.

used with misbehavior (see Chapter 5), while positive reinforcement should be used for encouraging good behavior.

1. Praise and Encouragement

There are many ways to praise and encourage a child, and there are many opportunities to do this every day. Too often, praise is the missing element in parent-child relationships. This is especially true with children who frequently misbehave. Parents concentrate on the child's faults and overlook his good behavior. Parents may think they frequently praise their children, but research suggests that many parents actually give very little praise and encouragement.

All people like to hear good things about themselves, and children are no exception. The self-esteem of a child is constantly developing, and kids really crave their parent's attention. It is difficult to underestimate what powerful tools praise and encouragement can be.

Praise can be directed toward a child's behavior ("I like the way you're sharing with your brother"). Praise can also be directed toward the child's self-esteem ("you're special," and "we love you"). Any praise that is not directly related to a particular behavior can be a self-esteem booster.

There are many ways to praise children including:

Expressing confidence ahead of time. Telling a child that you know she can do something is encouraging and can help build self-confidence.

Praising for effort. The child's effort is praised regardless of the outcome. When children try things, we should support them and we should not praise only when they "do it right."

Praising for accomplishment. Parents can praise when a child finishes a task. This could be anything from making the bed or getting his homework done, to spending half an hour cooperating with a brother or sister.

Involving others in praise. There are two ways this can be done. 1) You can praise your child when others are standing by to hear. 2) You can tell another person about your child's accomplishments while the child is nearby ("Hey, did you just see what a nice thing Sarah did?"). This can get a child very excited because she recognizes that you really appreciate her.

Using physical praise. Facial expression, voice inflection, eye contact, and posture can all express to your child that you appreciate his efforts at behaving appropriately. Also, a hand on the shoulder, a hug, or a kiss can convey to your child that you value his good behavior.

It is important that when parents praise, it be done in a genuine way. Never mix praise and insult. Many parents praise and insult at the same time ("Gee Brian, thanks for making your bed . . . it's about time!"). Children will recognize such comments as insults, not praise.

You should say something nice to your child almost any time he does something you appreciate. It does not have to be an important or significant behavior. It can be a little thing like thanking him for taking his plate from the table to the sink after dinner (even though you have said it a thousand times). If you wait around for your child to do the dishes on his own you will never allow yourself the opportunity to use praise!

Examples of praise and encouragement:

◊ Mom tells Justin how much she appreciates it when he shares his Nintendo with his little sister.
◊ Janelle's mom tells her how special she is.
◊ With his hand on his son's shoulder, Andrew's father thanks him for picking up all of the toys in the yard (even though he was reminded to clean up).
◊ After a weekend stay at grandma's house, Amanda's mother said "we really missed you. Things weren't much fun with you gone."
◊ Even though his bed spread was not very neat, Kevin's mother praises him for his efforts at making his bed.

2. Activity reinforcers

Activities that your kids enjoy can be used as incentives to help improve behavior. Rewards for positive behavior can include fun activities, games, outings, privileges, responsibilities, or anything else they may enjoy. Examples can include car trips, playing games with parents, helping a parent with some "grown-up jobs" (e.g., making cookies or washing the car together), going to a sporting event, renting a video, going shopping, etc. The list of activities your child enjoys is probably longer than you imagine. You can apply positive reinforcement for good behavior by using activities to reward your child. The reason your child is getting the reinforcement should always be made clear so he can make the connection between the good behavior and the reward.

Reinforcers should match the level of the behavior. Small behaviors should be followed by small reinforcers, and bigger reinforcers follow bigger accomplishments. For example, it would be absurd to say "Great Kevin, you were so good about making your bed this week, we're going to take you to Disney World!" Or how about, "Wow Jennifer, you've kept your room spotless for a month and improved all your grades on your report card, so you can stay up a half hour later tonight." Kevin would be confused, and Jennifer would be disappointed.

The Mystery Activity Approach. One clever way to use activity reinforcers is with the Mystery Activity. Once you have chosen a behavior to improve, you can use a mystery activity to reinforce your child for a day's worth of successful behavior. You will need to compile a list of 8 to 20 fun activities you know your child would enjoy. Then, she is rewarded with one of them following the good behavior. Not letting your child know which activity will be used as a reward has two advantages. The "mystery" aspect adds to the child's interest. It's like a wrapped present. Second, if the child knows that the day's activity reward is something she is not so interested in at the moment, it will not motivate her. The mystery element will keep her motivated. An alternative approach would be to compile a list of 8 to 20 activities and have your child select the one she wants as a reward.

One final note on activity reinforcers. As mentioned before, children crave their parent's attention. Activities that involve parents with their child are like a double reinforcement. If you invest more of your time and positive attention, and you will see better results.

Examples of activity reinforcers:

◊ Because Brendan was cooperative at the store, his mom let him help make cookies when they got home.

◊ After dinner, Kevin and his dad played a video game because Kevin cleared off the kitchen table and stacked the dishes by the sink.

◊ Andrea's parents are renting her a video after the first time she cleaned her room without being asked.

◊ Just prior to bedtime, Robert and Tommy were playing so well together (they usually fight), their mom said they could stay up a little later.

3. Material reinforcers

Material reinforcers can be used as incentives. However, they are not as natural as praise and activity reinforcers. Material reinforcers should always be kept small, unless you are using a token system (described below). A child can be told that if she behaves a certain way, she can receive a small reward. This could range from a cookie to some (very) small toy. The reason your child is getting the reinforcement should always be made clear to her. This will help her make the connection between the good behavior and the reward.

The behavior you are trying to improve should be the only way for your child to get the reward. If she will be able to get the same or similar reward through other means, the reward will lose its ability to motivate.

Bribes vs. Rewards. There are differences between "bribes" and rewards. Parents often think they are bribing their children to behave when they use a reward. But a reward is a way to show your child you appreciate his efforts at good behavior. It provides an incentive for future good behavior.

Parents are in control of rewards. By contrast, the child is in control of a "bribe." If the parent asks a child to shovel the snow from the driveway, and the child asks how much he is going to get for it, then that is a bribe. However, if the parent initiates the situation, it is not a bribe (e.g., "you can have a snack when your homework is finished"). If a parent uses a "reward" to get a child to behave once a misbehavior has started, this is a bribe. For example, if a child is misbehaving in a store and you tell him he will get a treat if he behaves the remainder of the time at the store, that is a bribe. This will teach the child to misbehave in the store so that you will pacify him with a treat! But if the parent explained *prior* to going to the store that he could earn a treat for good behavior, then that is a reward, not a bribe. There is no misbehavior being reinforced in this situation. If the parent decides something ahead of time, it is a reward. If the child sets the terms, it is a bribe.

A good rule of thumb is to rely on praise, encouragement, and activity reinforcers first (these are also called "social reinforcers"). Save material reinforcement for special situations, when the social reinforcers are not likely to work.

Examples of material reinforcers:
◊ Tanya was told she could choose any candy bar at the checkout counter if she did not argue at the store (she is usually a problem at the store).
◊ Aaron was told he could have hot cocoa and cookies for a snack if he helped his dad shovel snow from the driveway.
◊ Sarah was given a dollar for helping out at mom's yard sale.
◊ Dad gave Meghan a colored pencil each time she helped weed the flower garden.
◊ Whenever David finished his homework, he got to select a snack.

4. Token Reinforcers

A token reinforcer motivates a child while she is "earning" a larger reward that she will receive at a later time. For example, each time Jessica cleans her room, her mother drops a marble into a small glass jar. As soon as the jar is filled, she will

get to take a trip to the zoo. By itself, there is nothing reinforcing about dropping a marble into a jar. But when a child
recognizes that each marble means she is closer to her goal, the
marbles begin to motivate. Another idea is a chart on the wall.
A homemade drawing like a large thermometer can be used.
Each time the desired behavior is done, another section of the
thermometer can be colored in. When all the sections have been
colored in, the child receives the reward. Tokens can be used to
earn either activity reinforcers or material reinforcers. You
should always make it clear to your child why he is getting the
reinforcement so he can make the connection between the good
behavior and the reward.

If you have any question about whether token reinforcement can motivate people, consider the fact that our entire
economy is based upon tokens (cash, checks, credit cards) which
can be exchanged for things (merchandise, food, activities, etc.).

When using a token approach, do not remove tokens when
your child misbehaves. When he misbehaves, use one of the
techniques to reduce misbehavior presented in the next chapter.
Once a child has earned a token, he can get very discouraged
about the token approach if he starts losing tokens. A child
might lose motivation to earn tokens if he thinks they might be
taken away again. It may be best to keep approaches designed
to reduce misbehavior separate from approaches designed to
increase good behavior.

The behavior you are trying to improve should be your
child's only way to get a token (or the larger reward). If the
child will be able to get a token through other means, it will
lose its ability to motivate.

A difficulty arises when you are about to deliver on the
reinforcement, and the child misbehaves. For example, your
child has earned a trip to Pizza Hut using a token approach.
While you are getting ready to go, she smacks her brother, or
maybe she throws a big tantrum. Should you still take her to
the pizza shop? The answer is "yes," and "no." She should not

lose what she has earned. However, you do not want to let her think that she can get away with hitting or throwing a tantrum. In this situation, you have at least two logical choices. First, you could punish the behavior in a way that is unrelated to the pizza reward (e.g., have her sit on a chair for 10 minutes before you leave). Second, if the misbehavior was serious enough, you may need to tell your child, "I know you earned the trip to Pizza Hut, and I am not going to let you miss that. But you need to learn that you cannot hit your brother and expect us to take you somewhere special. We will have to go for pizza tomorrow night." You do not want to accidentally send the wrong message by giving a reward immediately following a misbehavior.

Examples of token reinforcers:
◊ Every night that Michael finishes his homework before supper, he gets to color in a space on a chart. When he has ten colored in, his parents will take him to his favorite pizza shop.
◊ Gina gets one sticker each morning she makes her bed before going to school. Whenever she gets 5 stickers, she gets to rent a video.
◊ Every day, Danny earns a check mark for completing each of his three daily chores. When Danny earns fifteen check marks, he gets to pick out a model car or airplane.
◊ Erin gets a smiley face drawn on a chart on the refrigerator each time she comes the first time she is called. When she gets ten smiley faces, she gets to pick out a favorite dessert.

5. Modeling

One of the most effective ways of creating or maintaining a good behavior is by making sure you consistently behave the way you expect your children to behave. This is called *modeling*. Children often behave like their parents because they use their parents' behavior as a model for theirs. If you do not want your children watching too much TV, consider how much TV you are watching. Many parents do not want their children to lie, yet they lie in front of their children all the time.

For example, the phone rings and the father says, "If it's for me, tell them I'm not home." The child learns that you can lie to avoid doing something you do not want to do. Parents complain about their children yelling all the time, yet they see their parents frequently yell and speak disrespectfully. Parents need consistency between their words and their *own* behavior. The old saying "practice what you preach" is so important with children. The adage "do as I say — not as I do," is a foolish way to deal with children. *Children pick up both good habits and bad habits from their parents. It is important that parents consistently behave in a way that their children can imitate.*

Another way to use modeling is to allow one of your children to see you compliment one of your other children when they display good behavior. This may help the other child to recognize what you expect and hopefully to model their behavior accordingly.[3]

It is also important for parents to realize the negative effect that television can have on children from the standpoint of modeling. Lying, cheating, violence, illicit sex, and disrespect of parental authority are all part of an average evening of prime time television. Much research has shown that kids are affected by this constant barrage of negative role models. Parents must stop using the TV to keep their kids occupied, and carefully monitor (and limit) what their children are watching. Otherwise, TV can actually hinder your efforts at helping your child develop better behavior.

Examples of modeling:
- ◊ A mom makes it a point to always say "please" and "thank you" to foster this habit in her children.
- ◊ Samantha's mother is going to be extra patient to help Samantha develop more patience.
- ◊ Timmy's father and mother are taking special caution to listen carefully and not interrupt when someone is talking because Timmy is having difficulty with these.

---

[3]This must be done in a natural manner to be successful. It will not work if this is done in a way whereby siblings feel they are being compared.

◊ A mother and father decide to stop using curse words and profanity because they do not want their children using them.

◊ Joey's parents decide not to raise their voices at their children or at each other because Joey has become a real yeller.

6. Practice

A good way to supplement modeling is practice. Kids can learn to develop good habits by repeated practice until the behavior becomes routine. For example, a parent may want to get her children to clear their area of the table after dinner. Each night, she reminds them, and they all bring their plate, etc. over to the sink. Reminders are nightly (unfortunately parents hate reminding so they do not give their kids enough practice). Eventually, parents wean the children off of constant reminders, but sometimes this is not necessary because with many opportunities for practice, it may eventually become a natural part of a child's routine.

Often parents assume the child can do a task because they have done it successfully once or twice. But just because a child was successful once or twice does not mean the child has "mastered" the task. If the child has not mastered the task, it is harder for him, and he will avoid it when asked. Practice may help to prevent this problem.

A helpful way for children to practice certain social skills is through *role playing*. This involves children practicing how they should behave while adults and siblings help act out the situation. If done in a game-like fashion, children can have fun while they are learning appropriate behavior.

Examples of practice:

◊ Mrs. Brown takes a few minutes a day to oversee her two children playing with their toys. She has them practice sharing. It sometimes seems awkward and artificial, but the children become more accustomed to sharing. Now they know more specifically what their mom means when she tells them to share.

◊ Every morning, Mr. Spencer oversees the children making their beds. When they need help, he shows them how to do it, then lets them try it themselves. As time goes on, Mr. Spencer spends less time overseeing the process, and eventually does not need to.

◊ Matthew's parents play a little game with him where they "role play" or "play act" different situations. During these situations, Matthew learns proper social behavior ranging from remembering to say "please," "thank you," and "excuse me," to learning how to introduce himself and take turns in a conversation.

7. Self-monitoring

Self-monitoring refers to the practice of having a child keep track of a certain behavior. When people keep track of their own behavior, they are more conscious of their behavior, and this promotes improvement. Self-monitoring may not work well alone (see combining reinforcers, below), but can be a helpful extra in improving behavior. A child may be asked to keep track of every time she puts her laundry in the hamper, or every time she makes her bed, or some other responsibility. Some children will do better at keeping track than others, but it may be worth a try with your child.

Self-monitoring may be used with a reward. If you use self-monitoring this way, you may want to oversee the accuracy of your child's records. If you keep an eye on his records, your child will be less likely to exaggerate in order to receive a reward. With many children, self-monitoring can work without a separate reward, especially if used with a behavior that the child agrees he wants to change.

Examples of self-monitoring:
◊ Jake keeps a simple record of when he does his homework each night.
◊ Trisha records each time she sets the table for dinner.
◊ Sean marks a chart each time he feeds the dog.
◊ Kyle keeps a running log of when he makes his bed.
◊ Katie's parents have designed a log which they have taped to the refrigerator. It covers three behaviors that should be part of Katie's afternoon routine. When she gets home from school, she

must hang up her coat, put away her book bag, and change her clothes. There is a spot on the chart for each of these three behaviors every day.

8. *Humor*

Humor can be an important tool to motivate good behavior. Good-natured jesting, joking, and kidding can help you get your child "on your side." Parents who always deal with their children in a very serious way can miss many opportunities to develop a positive, mutually enjoyable relationship. When I consult with parents who have children with behavior problems, I often find that the element of humor is missing. They no longer laugh together. People who can laugh together can learn more quickly to enjoy each other's presence. A little levity and light-heartedness can really spice up a parent-child relationship.

I've wondered if this may be one of the reasons why our children often seem to behave better for friends or relatives than for us. These other adults are perceived by our children as good natured and fun, while our children look at us as nags or as hostile. By using humor and spending much positive, affirming time with our children, we can try to help them see that we can be fun to be with.

It must be remembered that humor with children should always be respectful toward the child. It is unfortunate that most of the humor that is modeled for us on television "family" sitcoms is of the "put-down" variety. Humorous put-downs can take their toll on a child and must be avoided. The purpose of using humor with children is to promote a better relationship, not to get a few laughs at someone's expense.

Examples of using humor:

◊ Dad knows that Jason does not like to get ready for bed. A few minutes prior to the time Jason is to get ready for bed, Dad approaches Jason. The two talk, joke around, and get involved in some general silliness. Dad's approach lowered Jason's resistance level prior to being asked to get ready for bed. When the time comes, Jason is more cooperative.

◊ Because mom spends plenty of time demonstrating to Sarah that she is good natured and flexible, Sarah is more cooperative when she sees that mom is serious about a certain request.

Combining reinforcers

When reinforcements are combined, behavior is more likely to improve. Combining reinforcers can also change behaviors more quickly. Parents can use any combination of praise, activity reinforcers, material reinforcers, a token system, modeling, practice, self monitoring, and humor to effectively change behavior. Too often parents try one little strategy and are discouraged when it fails. Then they try something else, and it fails too. Eventually they try several things, none of which seem to work. If the parents had only tried a few things *in combination,* and kept it up for a a few weeks, they would have had better results.

Examples of combining reinforcers:

◊ While doing his homework, Timmy is provided with verbal praise, material reinforcers (cookies), and an activity reinforcer (he can play Nintendo or watch TV afterward).

◊ Cari's parents are using self-monitoring, a token approach (based upon her self-monitoring records), and verbal praise to help her develop the habit daily making the bed and clearing the floor of toys and clothes in her room.

◊ Using praise, activity reinforcers, and humor, Mr. and Mrs. Sweeney have helped their children develop many good habits, including brushing their teeth, getting dressed by themselves, and getting ready for bed when asked.

Avoidance Reinforcers

Sometimes negative things can motivate good behavior. In other words, a child can choose to display proper behavior to avoid something negative. When a child rides her bike, she is careful in order to avoid falling. A child might hurry up and finish her homework in school so she does not have to bring it home. One boy's father is going fishing, and the boy cannot go along unless his room is clean, so he cleans it. In each case, the child does not do the good behavior because he wants to. He does it to avoid something negative, whether it is falling from a bike or missing a fishing trip. These motivators are called *avoidance reinforcers*. This is because the child's behavior is reinforced when they successfully avoid something negative. For example, if the child successfully avoids having to bring homework home, she is more likely to continue working responsibly in school to avoid bringing the work home in the future. If the boy makes the fishing trip, he will learn that he can avoid missing such outings by finishing his chores.

Parents often use the threat of punishment as an avoidance reinforcer. They tell their child that if he does not display a particular good behavior, he will be punished. This is generally not a good practice because it puts too much emphasis on punishment and coercion to get children to comply. Punishment should be reserved for dealing with misbehavior, not for motivating good behavior. Using punishment to teach responsibility and good behavior can result in the child resenting the parent, and can put unnecessary strain on the parent-child relationship. If you want to increase a good behavior, you should use either a positive approach, or an acceptable form of avoidance reinforcement. Below are some ways parents can use avoidance to motivate in a constructive way.

1. The 'First Things First' Principle

One approach to using avoidance is as old as the hills. It involves ordering a child's activities so that fun activities follow not-so-fun activities. An example would be telling your child that he can play with his Nintendo only after he has cleaned his room. He sees one as an unwanted task, and the other as very desirable. The only way he can escape from the one situation is to do what is required (clean the room). This is a common approach that parents use. *However, this approach fails because parents let their children off the hook and do not hold them to the original agreement* (i.e., no Nintendo until the room is clean). If you are not consistent here, your child will learn to manipulate the situation by arguing and complaining until mom or dad gives in or compromises.

Examples of the "first things first" principle:

◊ Before Greg can go out and play with his friends, he has to finish his homework.

◊ If Tiffany wants to watch TV before school, she has to be dressed and have her school bag packed and ready to go.

◊ Kyle will not be able to go to soccer practice until his room is clean.

◊ Stephanie will not be served any dessert unless she has at least two forkfulls of vegetables.

2. The Hot Seat Approach

The *hot seat approach* is a way of dealing with outright defiance. For example, you ask your child to do some small, reasonable chore, and he stomps his foot and flatly refuses. After politely explaining to him that he should do what you asked, he still refuses. You decide you *must* get him to do what you asked or he will learn that he can avoid doing things by giving you a big hassle. You decide to use the hot seat approach. With this approach, you calmly and politely tell your child that he will have to sit on a chair (away from TV, toys, or anything else that could amuse him) until he does what you asked him to do. You stress that he is free to leave the chair at any time, just so long as he does what you asked him to do. You are not keeping him in the chair, he is keeping himself there by refusing to do what you asked.

The hot seat should only be used with requests which the child can easily fulfill, and are reasonable for his age. Typically, it should be used when your child refuses to do something that is his responsibility (e.g., picking up toys, cleaning up a spill).

The issue is dealing with the child's refusal, not with trying to get him to do some important job. This approach should only be used in situations of outright defiance.

Because your child is in full control of when to get out of the chair, you do not set a time limit. If you set a time limit, your child may learn to wait you out. If you are going somewhere soon, do not use this approach because you will not be able to see it through. When using the hot seat approach, the child might think he would rather sit in a chair than do what you say. However, after a while he will realize that he could be in the chair for a very long time, and that a little cooperation can get him out of the situation. When the child is being defiant, he is not just trying to avoid work, *he is trying to assert his authority over yours.* Therefore, it is vitally important for you to speak to your child in a calm, polite fashion in order to avoid building more antagonism. This will allow him a better atmosphere to humbly recognize that it is in his best interest to do what he was told. The hot seat may need to be done several times consistently before your child learns it is better to do what you say than to refuse.[4]

Examples of the hot seat approach:
◊ Stephen refused to help pick up the toys that were all over the living room. He had to sit in a chair until he decided he would help with the toys.
◊ Mom politely asked Rebecca to bring in her bike and doll house from the front yard, but she refused. Rebecca had to sit on mom's bed until she decided she would do what she was asked to do.
◊ Karen carelessly spilled Kool-Aid all over the kitchen floor. Her father politely handed her a sponge to clean it up. She refused to do it, even after two polite requests. The spill sat waiting for Karen until she decided to get off the chair to clean it up.

---

[4]Caution must be used with the *hot seat* approach because your child may try to outlast you — until you give in. You must not let this happen.

3. *The Group Effort Approach*

Another way to motivate children to do good behavior is through positive peer pressure. This can be created by parents using the *group effort approach*. With this approach, siblings are expected to work together to receive a group reward. The idea is that no one gets the reward unless each child does what you expect. For example, a parent may say that everyone's bed must be made before any of them can go out and play. The ones who have done their job will put pressure on the reluctant one to take care of his responsibility. Parents can get the others to *encourage* the reluctant one, in order to avoid a negative scene. It is obvious that this could backfire in instances where poor sibling relationships would undermine how well it works. However, in most family situations, it is worth a try.

Examples of the group effort approach:
◊ Every child in the family will receive an edible treat when their beds are made. However, no one gets a treat until all three children have made their bed.
◊ Before the family goes on their trip to the zoo, each child must have his or her teeth brushed and room straightened.
◊ The family will rent a video once each child has done her chores and finished her homework.

4. *The Gotcha Game*

The *Gotcha Game* teaches responsible behavior by using avoidance, but presented in a positive way. For example, a family could play a game dealing with making their beds in the morning. If someone in the family (parents included) neglects to make his or her bed, then the next day everyone gets their bed made by the forgetful person. With parents involved, the Gotcha Game can build morale with the kids. The kids will want to watch closely to see if they can catch mom or dad forgetting the expected chore. This way, the children will remember to do their part, because they want to avoid making all of the beds the next day. Parents should allow themselves to get "caught" soon after the plan begins in order to help the children get excited about the game. The Gotcha Game increases good behavior because the child is trying to avoid something negative (i.e., making all the beds, or whatever behavior you are working on). Because it is a game, it must be done in a good natured fashion. However, you must still be firm and consistent or else the Gotcha Game will not work.

Examples of the Gotcha Game:

◊ In one home, the children kept leaving things out of the refrigerator. The parents made a rule that if anyone left something out of the refrigerator, they had to stand next to the refrigerator and count out loud to twenty. Then, the parents purposely let their children catch them to get the "game" rolling. After about one incident each, the kids began to remember. It was not much of a punishment, but it did help them remember.

◊ In another home, whenever anyone forgot to take their plate, glass, and silverware to the sink after dinner, they had to clear the table of everyone's things the next night. Dad purposely "forgot" to do it the first night to get the kids interested in the new "game."

SUMMARY

A wide variety of reinforcers can be used to make a positive impact on your child's behavior, limited only by your time, willingness, and creativity. You can reinforce positively by praise, activity reinforcers, material reinforcers, a token approach, modeling, practice, self-monitoring, humor, or some combination of these. You can also motivate through avoidance by seeing to it that your child does first things first, by using the hot seat, the group effort approach, or the Gotcha Game. Using combinations of reinforcers, both positive reinforcement and avoidance, can be an effective way to improve your child's behavior.

Chapter 5

How to Reduce Misbehavior

In this chapter you will learn:
- ◊ Over a dozen different strategies you can use to decrease your child's misbehavior.
- ◊ How to reduce misbehavior by making the cost of the misbehavior too high.
- ◊ How to reduce misbehavior by removing the child's incentive for misbehaving.
- ◊ How to combine strategies to reduce misbehavior more effectively.

There are two ways to reduce misbehavior. One way is to make the cost of the misbehavior too high. In other words, you provide negative consequences to your child expecting that these consequences will outweigh the benefits he receives from misbehaving. There are a variety of negative consequences described below. The second way to reduce misbehavior is to remove the child's incentive for misbehaving. This recognizes the fact that a child is motivated to misbehave *for a reason*. If you can remove that motivation or incentive, you will see the misbehavior decrease. There are several types of "incentive removal" strategies described in the second half of this chapter.

There is no suggestion that every parent will want to use all of the strategies presented in this chapter. Different parents will feel comfortable using different approaches. It is important to use methods you feel comfortable with. Nothing will undermine your efforts more than half-hearted attempts with an approach you feel uncomfortable using.

Important Note: If you skipped ahead to this chapter because you wanted to discover ways of dealing with misbehavior, go back and read Chapter 3 before you try use the following strategies. The techniques in this chapter *will not be helpful* if they are not used properly. Chapter 3 - *Keys to Improving Behavior* teaches how to use behavioral principles in a way that will make them effective.

Negative Consequences

Negative consequences can be used to decrease or eliminate misbehavior. Consequences should be made clear in advance. Whenever possible, consequences should be applied *each time the misbehavior occurs*. Once a consequence has been given, you must not back down until it has run its course. If you tell your child he cannot go out for the rest of the evening because he misbehaved, do not compromise if he suddenly begins to display better behavior.[1] This will teach your child not to take you seriously when you give consequences. He will become more persistent in getting you to compromise any punishment. Once a punishment has run its course, your child will have plenty of opportunities to demonstrate good behavior and be reinforced for it.

When properly applied (see Chapter 3), negative consequences can reduce or eliminate misbehavior. However, only positive incentives and a positive relationship with parents will motivate a child's good behavior. If parents only rely on the information presented in this chapter, they will miss many of the positive aspects of discipline described in Chapters 4 and 8. It is important to avoid the downward spiral of relying too much on punishment. However, when kept in balance, the techniques described below can be important resources to help

---

[1]See the sections "Less is More" and "The 24 Hour Rule" in Chapter 3 to find ways of keeping punishments brief so that there is less opportunity for your child to convince you to compromise.

parents deal with misbehavior. With discipline, consequences and punishment are only half the picture. Successful discipline involves developing a more positive rapport with your child.

Your child's mood may have a big effect upon how well consequences work. I have heard of many "stand-off" situations where parents continued to pile consequence upon consequence while the child resisted or kept saying, "I don't care." This should be avoided. When it becomes clear that a child is too upset to reason clearly, or is standing his ground because of pride or to "save face," it is better to shift from a consequence approach to an incentive removal approach. For example, Devin was very upset at his brother so he took and hid one of his brother's favorite toys. His parents demanded he return it immediately or he would lose TV privileges for the night. Devin refused, so his parents told him that he lost TV and next would lose his Nintendo for the evening. Devin continued to resist, and his parents kept adding to the punishment, even going into extra days of punishment. Devin was very upset, and his parents failed to recognize that their attempts to punish did not mean anything to Devin at the moment. They should have changed their approach once it was clear he was upset and the withdrawal of TV did not seem to work. The *hot seat* approach[2] or one of incentive removal techniques described later in the chapter may have been more helpful than using a negative consequence. In many situations, negative consequences will not be the most effective way to reduce misbehavior.

1. Natural Consequences

Natural consequences occur as the natural result of a behavior. For instance, a child rides his bike recklessly and he falls and gets hurt. He is mean to his friends and he loses friends. He forgets to bring his lunch to school so he goes hungry until he gets home.

---

[2]This was described in the previous chapter.

Parents cannot control natural consequences, but there are ways to make use of them when they do occur. The first way is for parents to allow the natural consequences to occur! Parents should not protect their child from natural consequences (so long as the consequences will not cause harm). For example, if John forgets his lunch once, there is nothing wrong with mom or dad running his lunch to school. But if this is something he does regularly, John's parents would be doing him a disservice if they kept bringing his lunch to school. They would be preventing him from experiencing the natural consequences of his irresponsibility, and not allowing John a valuable learning opportunity. Parents should certainly protect their child from harm, but when natural consequences are not harmful (and most are not), parents should allow these circumstances to teach responsible behavior.

A second way parents can make use of natural consequences is to calmly and respectfully explain to the child how their behavior resulted in the misfortune. Steven fell off his bike after trying to do a daring stunt. Steven's dad helped him up, put his arm around Steven to comfort him and calm him down. Then he talked to him about the consequences of doing dangerous things with his bike. Thus, even though Steven's dad did not cause the natural consequence, he used the incident to teach Steven about responsible bike riding. His calm respectful approach avoided the "I told you so" attitude which Steven would have tuned out.

Examples of natural consequences:

◊ Alex was told many times to stay out of the neighbor's tree. When Alex fell from the tree and skinned his knee, his dad respectfully (i.e., without an "I told you so" attitude) explained to Alex how his behavior led to the accident.

◊ After a few mild bullying incidences, two of Danny's friends told him they did not want to play with him anymore. Danny's mom helped him learn how his bullying affected his friends' desire to play with him.

◊ Cari was running quickly up the stairs and fell. After being comforted by her mom, the two discussed an appropriate speed for going up the stairs.

2. Logical Consequences

Logical consequences do not naturally result from an action. However, unlike many types of punishment, logical consequences are *related* to the misbehavior. Michael rides his bike where he is not supposed to, he is then not allowed to ride his bike for the rest of the day. Kimberly and Danny fight over the Nintendo, so the Nintendo gets put away for the night. Andrea carelessly walks through the house with her boots on, so she has to clean up the trail of dirt she left behind. In each case, the child is held accountable for his or her action, and the consequence is related to the act. After experiencing logical consequences several times, a child will usually learn to avoid that behavior in the future.

Logical consequences can be used for accidental and careless behavior as well as defiant misbehavior. Expecting children to clean up their own spills (or at least "help" if they are very young) can influence them to be more careful. Yelling or lecturing usually does not help a child to be more careful. A logical consequence is the most useful way to decrease an undesirable behavior, either accidental or purposeful. Unfortunately, with some misbehavior, it is not possible to find a suitable logical consequence, so some other approach is necessary. However, logical consequences should be the first type of consequence a parent should use, whenever possible.

Logical consequences are probably the best teaching tools because there is a direct relationship between the misbehavior and the consequence. This way, your child will be more likely to make the association, and will be less likely to associate the consequence with your mood. Remember, every effort should be made to use logical consequences as the first response to misbehavior. When there is either; 1) no suitable logical consequence, or 2) when *consistent* use of a logical consequence does not prove effective you would need to consider the other alternatives described below.

Examples of logical consequences:
◊ Peter left his lunch home for the third time in one month. His dad decided to stop dropping it off at school to help him learn to be responsible.
◊ Steven and Jessica kept fighting over the Atari one afternoon, so their dad said that it would be turned off until after dinner.
◊ Brendan was disrupting everyone's dinner, so he had to finish his dinner in another room.
◊ Karen spilled her milk at the table, so she was asked to clean it up with a sponge, and pour another glass by herself.
◊ Twelve year old Todd came home one evening a half hour later than the time he and his parents agreed upon. The next night he had to stay at home for the evening.

3. Overcorrection

Overcorrection means that a child has to make restitution for his behavior, in some cases restoring the situation to better than it was before the incident of misbehavior. It is a more strict version of a logical consequence. Tim was caught writing on the wall. Not only was he expected to clean it off, but he also had to clean the whole wall. Overcorrection is best used when a logical consequence may not be enough to give the child a sense of his misbehavior. Also, overcorrection is more appropriate when the misbehavior is deliberate. The parent should carry out overcorrection in a respectful, non-demeaning way.

Examples of overcorrection:
◊ Karen was being silly at dinner and spilled the milk three times in one week. The previous two times, her parents simply had her clean it up and pour another glass (i.e., they were using a logical consequence). Because she did not seem to be getting the message, her mom decided that she had to clean up the spill, then clean the

whole table (and floor around the table) after dinner. In addition, she would not have any more milk that meal.

◊ In Greg's house there is a rule that no one can eat in the living room. Greg was caught in the living room with a cookie, and got crumbs on the floor. His father had Greg vacuum the whole living room carpet.

◊ Justin carelessly trampled through the next door neighbor's garden. Justin's mother immediately sent him back over to apologize to the neighbor, help repair what could be repaired, and to weed the garden.

4. Positive Practice

Positive practice is another form of overcorrection. When a child misbehaves, he has to practice the expected behavior. Jimmy ran in the house and slammed the door behind him, despite being told not to slam doors. Jimmy's mother made him go back over to the door, go in and out three times, each time closing the door quietly. Jimmy's mother was using positive practice. This "practice" allows Jimmy to think twice next time before slamming the door behind him. Jimmy's mom did not have him stand in one place and close the door three times just to punish him. That would be pointless and humiliating. Rather, she had him repeat the *whole process*, so that he really practiced doing the task properly.

I have had several parents come up with the idea of using positive practice to get their children to hang up their coats and put away their things when they get home from school. In each case, they had the child go back out the door with his or her coat on, and practice the process 2 to 3 times. Each parent was thrilled with how well positive practice worked. Another parent used it to get her son to talk more quietly. Whenever he spoke in an inappropriately loud voice (which was most of the time), he had to repeat it at a normal level. School teachers use this approach when they catch children running in the hall. By having the child start over again and walk down the hall correctly (one or more times), they get results.

Positive practice is effective for at least three reasons. First, children practice the correct behavior, so it increases the chance that the correct behavior will become a habit. Second, the little practice sessions call attention to the behavior in a way that causes the child to think twice about doing it properly the next time. Third, a child will want to behave properly to avoid future "practice sessions." Positive practice is an old technique that has been well researched yet it is not used very often by parents. It can work in a variety of situations, although it does not apply to many types of behavior.

Examples of positive practice:

◊ Amanda and Tiffany spent much time yelling at each other. Their parents decided that whenever the girls yelled, they had to repeat the dialog twice in a calmer tone, and with kinder words.

◊ Joshua kept leaving things out in the yard at night. So, whenever he came in for the night without bringing in his bike, toys, etc., his parents had Joshua "practice" clearing the yard. Two times he would clear the yard under his parents' supervision, each time replacing the toys for the next practice. The neighbors may have thought the family was looney, but Joshua quickly learned not to neglect this basic responsibility.

◊ Chad and Thomas often ran up the stairs loudly. Their parents were concerned about the boys safety and were annoyed by the noise. By now I'll bet you know what their parents did about it!

5. Isolation

Isolation is when a child is told to sit in a chair or go to his room as a consequence for misbehavior. Sending a child to his room is often ineffective for three reasons. First, the child can entertain himself with books, toys, maybe even a TV or video game. This kind of "punishment" is usually not effective. Second, parents often assign a child to his room for too long. Most children, especially young ones, will forget why they are being punished and will not make the connection between the misbehavior and the consequence. Imagine a typical scene: Dad arrives home and asks, "Where's Michael?" "He is in his room for hitting his sister," responds Mom. Dad goes upstairs where Michael has been for half an hour. Dad asks, "How come you were sent to your room?" Michael's response? "Because Mom was mad!"

Also, sending children to their room for long periods of time is usually not effective because parents have a hard time enforcing it. First, they do not like sending their child to his room for a long time because it seems so harsh, so they overlook misbehavior that they should otherwise deal with. Only when the parents reach their "boiling point" do they act. Also, kids plead with their parents until they decrease the punishment. This teaches the child that he can get off easy with a little effort.

A more effective use of isolation would be to have your child sit at the kitchen table, or a chair in the hall, or any other place where boredom prevails (because there are no toys, TV, other children, or entertainment of any sort). *Isolation* should only last about five minutes. Parents will be more willing to enforce the rule when it is only five minutes,[3] and the child is not there long enough to forget *why* he is there. Several times in the chair in an evening will help get your message across (even if it takes the child several evenings). The key is to use isolation for five minutes *every time he misbehaves*. An effective way to administer isolation is to use a kitchen timer that has a bell which goes off. Some may find that if they do a lot of cooking and have a lot of misbehavior to deal with, they may want to invest in two timers!

Some readers may wonder how isolation would work because you know your child would never stay in a chair. If your child will not stay in a chair, then you will have to "train" him to stay in the chair. In some cases this would mean

---

[3]If you think five minutes is too brief, read the section "Less is more" in Chapter 3. Ten minutes may be a better amount of time for children age 9 to 12. Some have suggested one minute for each year of the child's age (i.e., four minutes for a four year old, seven minutes for an seven year old, etc.).

restraining him in the chair for the full five minutes. If this is done conscientiously, the child will learn that he will be spending time in the chair when told, so it is not worth putting up a fight. At first you may need to stand next to the chair to make him comply. Even in this situation, you will be able to gradually back away after many chair incidences, as long as you are ready to take action to keep him in the chair if he decides to resist. As mentioned, if ever physical persuasion[4] is used with a child, safety must never be compromised.

Sending a child to his room has its place, but usually under different circumstances (see "Time Out" on page 76).

Examples of isolation:
◊ Erin had to sit on the living room couch for 5 minutes every time she began to argue with her mother.
◊ Dennis had to sit in a chair in the corner of the dining room for 5 minutes every time he yelled at anyone (his brother or parents).
◊ Janelle had to sit at the kitchen table for 5 minutes every time she was aggressive toward her sister.
◊ Every time Stephen began whining and crying to get his way, he had to sit in a chair in his parents' room for 5 minutes.

6. Response-Cost

Response-cost has been shown to to be highly successful for variety of situations. With this strategy a child loses something he could have, usually money. For example, Dad gives Jason $1 at the beginning of the week. Four quarters are taped to the refrigerator, or to dad's dresser. Jason is told that any night he comes in from playing outdoors five minutes after the street light comes on, one quarter will be removed. The number of quarters left at the end of the week are for Jason to keep. Money or some kind of token can be used. However, it seems best not to mix response-cost with a token reinforcement[5] approach.

---

[4]See Chapter 3 under the section called "Proximity."
[5]See the previous chapter.

Tokens earned as reinforcement should not be removed. If you use token reinforcement and response-cost, keep them separate. Also, you should not allow money or tokens to be earned back if they were lost due to response-cost. Your child must learn you are serious about following through, and he will have future opportunities to earn reinforcement via good behavior the next time you set up the response-cost program.

Examples of response-cost:
◊ Each day, Trisha's mom taped 4 nickels to the refrigerator. Each time Trisha gave her mother "back talk," one nickel was removed. Trisha could keep whatever money remained on the refrigerator at the end of the day.
◊ Ryan's mom taped ten quarters to a kitchen cupboard. Each time he used a word he was not supposed to use (including swear words or others like "jerk" and "idiot") a quarter was removed.
◊ Each time Robert and John began to fight or argue with each other, they lost a dime from a small jar (they started with about 15 dimes). At the end of three days, they could split whatever was left.

7. *Withdrawal of Privilege*

This is one of the most common consequences parents use with their children, although it is probably one of the least effective. If a child misbehaves, she will lose a privilege for some period of time (e.g., TV, a toy, an activity). If the withdrawal of the privilege is related directly to the misbehavior (e.g., child is not allowed a toy because he was misbehaving with it), then it would be a type of logical consequence. However, withdrawing a privilege may not be related to the misbehavior. Withdrawing a privilege will only work if it is something the child will really miss. Also, the consequences must be made clear by the parent ahead of time. Withdrawal of a privilege should ordinarily be of a short duration, usually not to exceed a 24 hour period.[6]

---

[6]See the section "The 24 Hour Rule" in Chapter 3.

Although this is one of the most common punishments used by parents. it should actually be one of the last approaches used, when none of the others would be appropriate. Withdrawing a privilege is usually not an immediate consequence, and therefore it takes children longer to learn the connection between behavior and consequence.[7] Use this approach sparingly. Nine times out of ten, one of the other approaches in this chapter will work better than withdrawing a privilege (except if the privilege is logically related to the misbehavior).

I would not recommend using early bedtime as a punishment. Many parents have enough trouble getting their kids to bed. If bedtime is used as a consequence, your child may associate bed with punishment. This can make regular bedtime more of a problem because your child will have a more negative attitude about bedtime than he already has.

Examples of withdrawal of privilege:

◊ Aaron lost an evening of television because he swore at his mother.

◊ Hannah did not get to go bowling with her brother and cousin because that afternoon she was caught pushing her little sister off a chair.

◊ Michael could not play with his video games for the rest of the evening because he told his mother he had finished his homework when he had not.

8. Spanking

Spanking is another form of negative consequence that many parents use to discipline their children. However, spanking has become quite a controversial topic. Opinions on the issue of spanking vary from total opposition to cautious acceptance. The current "politically correct" attitude is that spanking is always wrong. But like so many other issues, "political correctness" sees everything as black and white, while in the real world there are also shades of gray. Just because

[7]See the section on "Timing" in Chapter 3.

there are parents who physically abuse their children, it does not logically follow that a swat on the rear end of a 4 year old for running in the road is also child abuse. To be consistent, this politically correct mentality would have to favor a total ban on *all* alcohol use because alcohol abuse is so common.

Because there is no experimental research to guide our opinion, and because the non-experimental research that is available is open to different interpretations (usually based on one's preconceived notions), opinions are just that — opinions. Since there are well-informed, well-intentioned experts on both sides of this issue, it seems best to avoid being dogmatic about our attitudes regarding spanking. Let's all agree to be dogmatic about fighting child abuse, but let's not define child abuse so broadly that most American parents are therefore child abusers.

I cannot agree that spanking is always wrong. There have been too many families that have used this strategy responsibly without any indication of physical or psychological harm. For young children, from approximately age two to about six or seven, spanking can provide an immediate, meaningful (although not logical) consequence that can be associated with misbehavior. This is why many parents say it can be effective.

On the other hand, even though I believe spanking can, under the right conditions, be responsibly used by parents as part of a broader discipline plan, *I have never recommended spanking to parents!* This is because I have no way of knowing how such advice would be applied once it has left my office. If I recommended spanking, or even said I agreed with the practice, some parents who may be beating their kids might think they have my approval (people often hear what they want to hear). For this reason, I focus on the many other options open to parents which do not have the potentially negative "side effects" that spanking could have. In the same way, I challenge you, the reader, to consider ways that you can deal effectively with misbehavior without resorting to spanking.

My general recommendations are 1) If you don't spank, don't start. This book can show you ways to discipline effectively without spanking; 2) If you do spank, reconsider ways you could substitute other strategies in situations where you would ordinarily spank; 3) If you insist on using spanking, make sure it is only with younger children (maybe two to six), make sure you do not spank them anywhere except on the buttocks, make sure you only use your hand (no belts, or paddles, etc.), and make sure you are not angry or in a rage. Otherwise, in my opinion, you would be physically abusing your child. This last point may be the most important. There is a difference between a parent who uses spanking in a calm, controlled fashion, and a parent who tends to "fly off the handle" and smack his or her children around. When you mix hostility and anger with spanking, you end up with ineffective discipline, and a very high likelihood of child abuse.

A Final Thought On Negative Consequences

It is important to remember that not every technique mentioned above is well suited for all types of misbehavior. You should use *logical consequences* (including *positive practice* or *overcorrection*) whenever possible. When you do not find a logical consequence that is suitable, you can use one of the other approaches.

Sometimes, negative consequences are not the best way to deal with misbehavior. A different approach, based upon removing the incentive for misbehavior may be more appropriate. We will now look at this type of technique.

Incentive Removal

There are several techniques that can help reduce misbehavior by removing the child from the source of reinforcement. Children misbehave for a reason. They gain some benefit from misbehaving (or at least they think they are gaining something). If parents can take away whatever benefit a child receives from the misbehavior, they remove the child's motivation to misbehave. With the ideas described, you will not always need to find out what is motivating your child in order to get results.

1. Broken Record

The "broken record" technique is a very effective way to end arguments with your children. This approach is as old as the hills, but many parents do not use it, or they use it rarely or haphazardly. Most parents do not realize how effective the broken record can be when used properly. Here is how it works. A parent makes a statement or request, and when the child begins to argue, the parent simply repeats the statement, like a "broken record." The parent does this each time the child attempts to continue the argument. The child eventually gives up arguing because he realizes he is talking to a "brick wall."

For Example:
Mom: Justin, it's time to pick up your toys and get ready for bed.
Justin: But mom, I want to play longer.
Mom: (Calm but firm) Justin, I said pick up your toys.
Justin: Why can't I play longer, none of my friends go to bed this early.
Mom: (Still calm but firm) Justin, there'll be no arguing, pick up your toys, and get ready for bed.
Justin: But mom, I don't want to go to bed yet.
Mom: (Still calm but firm) Justin, I said no arguing. Pick up your toys, it's time for bed.
Justin: (Starting to put away toys) I don't get to do anything.

The broken record is best used when arguments are an ongoing problem (which is the case in many homes). Your kids think that if they can engage you in an argument, they can get out of doing what they were asked to do (or at least decrease what you expect from them). Parents are easily pulled into this kind of argument. As you know, it is almost impossible to "win" an argument with your child.

A child's arguing is reinforced when we argue back! By engaging the parent in an argument, the child is attempting to get his mom or dad to either 1) give in or back down, or 2) compromise. Kids learn that by arguing they can often manipulate their parents, so they usually give it a try. The broken record works because it removes the incentive for arguing. The parent does not back down, but holds firm to his or her statement. Children soon realize they are getting nowhere with their argument and eventually give up.

Many parents have told me their children hate it when they use the broken record technique. This is because it works. I have had parents tell me stories of how frustrated their children get when their parents use the broken record, and how their kids storm off and slam doors. This just means that the broken record is working. The results in some cases are incredible. I have had two different moms independently say to me the exact same words: "It has been like heaven around my house since I've been using the broken record."

When using the broken record, it is important that you *do not get drawn into the argument* once the child begins to argue. This is true even if the child says something false that you would like to correct. For example, your child may say, "you never let me do thus and such." Even though you know that is not true, do not try to explain to your child that he is incorrect. *If you do, you have been drawn into the argument and he begins to gain ground.* Even comments like "you don't love me" or "how come you keep saying the same thing over and over?" must be met with "Justin, I said pick up your toys, and get ready for bed." At a later time, when he is not trying to argue, you will have a chance to correct his statements.

This approach does not excuse parents from communicating and listening to their children. However, once a child has had an explanation, it is not necessary to keep explaining to him over and over again just because he asks "why." Justin's mom had told him several times in the past when his bedtime was, and why it was important for him to get his rest. But Justin always asked "why" whenever mom made a request. Justin's mom should not give lengthy explanations whenever he asks her why he has to go to bed. He has been told why, and either he cannot understand, or does not agree with her explanations. *Further explanations will not help!* Because mom kept giving him the same response (like a "broken record"), he was not getting the benefit he was looking for (i.e., an argument which he knows might result in extra playtime).

From my experience, I find that parents often rely too much on giving kids lengthy explanations for things. Parents are then disappointed that their children do not comply. Kids respond much better to action than to lectures. A child always deserves an explanation — the first time, and maybe even the second time. After that, a technique such as the broken record should be used to stop the arguing. You will be amazed at the results if this is consistently applied to your child's arguing behavior.

If you use the broken record approach and your child will not comply after you have repeated yourself 5 to 8 times in a row, then you should inform him that there will be a negative consequences if he continues to argue (such as being sent to his room or sit in a chair).

It is important to remember that the broken record technique is best suited to end arguments, and does not guarantee the child will do something you ask. One parent informed me that the broken record did not work. She explained that she told her son that he could not watch his TV in his bedroom when he went to bed anymore, except on weekends. He began to argue and she used the broken record. He gave up arguing when he realized he was talking to a brick wall. That night, he quietly turned on his TV after he went to bed, in direct disobedience to his mother. Therefore, she concluded that the broken record did not work. I explained that the broken record worked perfectly. It stopped the argument, which is the purpose of using the broken record. She would need another approach to deal with the disobedience (like remove the TV from his room!). After ending an argument, parents may still have to back up their words with some other type of action to increase good behavior or decrease misbehavior.

For many parents, constant arguments are a problem in their home. The broken record is ordinarily the most effective way to end this problem.

Examples of the broken record:

◊ Every time Patrick argued to get something he could not have, his mother simply repeated that he could not have it, without giving him big explanations. She kept this up despite his attempts to draw her into the argument.

◊ Colleen argued every time her mother asked her to do something. To avoid the argument, Colleen's mom simply repeated her request until Colleen stopped arguing. If Colleen did not comply after the argument ended, her mother used the hot seat approach described in Chapter 4.

2. Planned Ignoring

Ignoring is commonly used by parents. The only problem is that ignoring must be done properly, or it can backfire resulting in worse behavior than you started with! Here is why this happens. For example, a boy pesters his mom for a cookie between meals and she says, "no." The boy keeps pestering, and mom keeps trying to ignore him. Because mom is trying to get something done in the kitchen, she finally says, "here, take this cookie, and don't bother me while I'm busy." What the child learns from this lesson is that if he keeps up the pestering long enough, mom will eventually give in. The child realizes that what used to take only two or three requests may now take many requests, and with a whiny voice as well! Because mom did not keep ignoring until the pestering stopped, she accidentally reinforced her child, and her plan backfired.

The only way for ignoring to work is for parents to decide to outlast their child by ignoring for as long as it takes, no matter what. Only then will they see improvement. The child realizes no matter how hard he tries to get what he wants, he is still going to be ignored. At that point the behavior will decrease. If a parent gives in, it will strengthen the misbehavior, or even make it worse. The important thing to remember is that ignoring must be carefully planned. *It will only work with behaviors that can be ignored no matter how bad it gets.* Parents and teachers say to me, "I try to ignore it, but then it gets so bad I have to do something." Getting a response from a parent, good or bad, may be enough to teach the child to be more persistent in their misbehavior.

Ignoring should not be used for general misbehavior. Ignoring can make the problem worse if the child misbehaves to get some benefit for misbehavior (besides parental attention). For example, if the child gets some benefit out of being aggressive toward other kids, ignoring that child will *not* decrease the behavior. *Ignoring only works when the purpose of the misbehavior is to attract the parent's attention or to get some response out of the parent.* Therefore planned ignoring should only be used when misbehavior meets *both* of the following conditions:

1) It is done to get a parent's attention (such as pestering, whining, and throwing tantrums), and

2) It can be ignored no matter how bad it gets.

In these situations, ignoring can be very effective. However, if the misbehavior you are dealing with does not fit *both* of these conditions, you should use a different strategy.

Examples of planned ignoring:

◊ Each time Andy threw a tantrum, his parents ignored him, no matter how loud he got. They would even walk out of the room so he would lose his "audience."

◊ Four year old Brendan constantly called for his parents after he was put to bed. It drove them crazy. Each time it was another request ("I want water," "fix my blanket," etc.). His parents decided that when they put him to bed they would take care of everything he usually asked for before leaving his room. Then they told him they would not return to his room for the night. Then, they ignored him when he called out for them. Eventually, Brendan stopped calling to them at night. He learned they were not going to respond. They had to "outlast" Brendan's yelling and crying for several nights before they saw improvement.

◊ Christi whined for everything. Her parents decided to ignore any statements by Christi which were accompanied by whining.

3. Time Out

Time out means removing a child from whatever is reinforcing a misbehavior. For example, if a child is upset, fighting, throwing tantrums, etc., sending him to another quiet place will remove him from the things that are agitating him. It will allow him the chance to calm down. For example, Shawn is a real show-off when his parents are entertaining their friends. These adults laugh at his silliness and generally pay much attention to him. Mom keeps saying things like, "Shawn, don't stand on the couch," "Shawn, don't bring your baseball bat in here," "Shawn, quit doing that to Uncle Jim." However, Shawn is too stimulated by the situation, so mom finally sends him to his room or outside to play where he is removed from what is reinforcing his misbehavior (i.e., the other adults).

If your child throws a tantrum, is fighting with siblings, showing off, etc., removing him from the situation can calm him down, because *it was the situation* that was agitating him. Once calm, you have a better chance to reason with your child and further discipline can be discussed if necessary.

Sending a child to his or her room seems to be a common punishment used by parents. But *time out* is somewhat different from *isolation* (discussed above). With *isolation,* your intention is to give your child a negative consequence for his misbehavior. With *time out,* you are trying to reduce the misbehavior by removing him from the source of the misbehavior (usually to calm him down). Time out does not need to be a punishment. However, in some situations, there is no distinction between *time out* and *isolation.*

One way to remember the difference between *time out* and *isolation* is by remembering where you send your child. With *isolation,* you send him to a boring spot (a chair or corner) to punish a misbehavior, usually for just a few minutes. With *time out,* you send him to his room (or simply out of the room he is currently in) to cool down because he was misbehaving due to excitement or aggravation. You do not care if he has fun while he is in time out. In his room he can read, play, etc. Your goal is to have him stay there until he feels he can come back less excited and in control of his behavior. Remember *isolation* is a negative consequence, *time out* means removing the child from the situation.

Examples of time out:

◊ Mom put Andrea in time out each time she became very excited and argumentative. After Andrea calmed down, they could talk.

◊ When Joshua and Jared got upset at each other, their dad would send them to separate rooms for a few minutes to "cool off."

◊ When Jake's friends or cousins come over, he gets very excited, silly, and misbehaves. His parents decided that when they saw him escalating, they would put him in time out for 5 minutes. Because they did not want to embarrass him in front of others, they would call him over and quietly tell him to go to a quiet place to cool down. He would simply mention to his friends, "I'll be back in a few minutes." His friends were not really aware what was going on. They did not think he was being corrected because they heard no yelling!

4. *Redirection (or Distraction)*

Redirection can be an effective solution in some situations, but it is only a temporary solution. Your child will not "learn" anything when you use it. However, it can be a helpful "quick fix" in some situations. This strategy involves the parent redirecting the child's attention away from the source of the misbehavior, and onto something more constructive.

If you notice that 1) your child is going through a series of misbehaviors, some rather bold and attention getting, and 2) you have not spent much positive time recently (i.e., in the last hour or two), then maybe you should set aside what you are doing and spend some time with your child. He may be trying to tell you he wants some of your time and attention. Instead of coming down harshly on him for all of the incidences of misbehavior, you may choose to use redirection. Even in situations where your child is not trying to get your attention by misbehavior, redirection can stop the downward spiral of misbehavior — punishment — more misbehavior — more punishment.

There is an important consideration with timing, however. You don't want your time and attention to become a reward for misbehavior. You may need some type of transition between the child's misbehavior and the constructive time you will spend with him. One way is to provide a small consequence for the most recent misbehavior. Then, soon after the consequence, tell the child "now we're going to do thus and such."

Examples of redirection:

◊ After Chris sat in a chair for the third time in the last hour, his dad set aside what he was doing and began to work together with Chris on a model airplane.

◊ Jeffrey's mom noticed he was getting aggravated because his older brother was using a toy he wanted and would not give him a turn. Jeffrey's mom asked Jeffrey to help her in another room with something Jeffrey enjoyed doing.

◊ One rainy day, Mrs. Johnson's three children were getting on each other's nerves. She took the initiative and the four of them played cards and board games for the afternoon.

5. Prevention

Prevention is a common practice that most parents use without thinking much about it. However, by giving it more thought, you may find better ways to use it. Like *redirection* described above, prevention can be effective, but is only a temporary solution. Your child is not likely to "learn" anything that will carry over to future situations. Regardless, prevention can save you from aggravation in a variety of circumstances.

Prevention involves setting up a situation with your child's misbehavior in mind. You design the situation so that your child *does not have the opportunity* to misbehave in the way you are concerned about. For example, if your child gets unmanageable when he has a few friends over, you may allow him to have only one or two friends over at a time. If he is always a problem at the grocery store, you may want to make arrangements so that he does not accompany you to the store. The idea is to think through the types of situations when your child displays the misbehavior. Then, you alter the situation so that he will not be able to misbehave that way. This is much like "child proofing" a home for a toddler. You remove all valuable and dangerous things or put them up high so that the toddler cannot hurt himself or damage property. Prevention means you remove the child from the opportunity to misbehave.

Prevention is a common practice among parents, but care must be taken that it is not overused. With prevention, children do not learn how to handle themselves when they have an opportunity to misbehave. Prevention can be helpful in situations where the parent needs a quick solution. Also, if a behavior is very persistent or troublesome, a parent can use prevention to tie them over until other alternatives can be used. Finally, it is best that prevention not be used like a punishment. For example, it would be inappropriate to say: "I'm never going anywhere with you until you can grow up and act civilized." You are not trying to punish or humiliate your child in these situations. You are simply not allowing him the chance to misbehave in the way you are concerned about.

Examples of prevention:

◊ Gina's mom would leave her with a friend when she shops for groceries. Because Gina was such a problem in the store, her mom did this while she was working on better behavior at home with Gina. It was not until she saw improvement in Gina at home that her mom felt confident enough to extend the principles of behavior management to the store as well.[8]

◊ One family routinely had very bad experiences on their many long car trips to visit family out of town. To avoid this they 1) got their family members to agree to visit *them* more of the time, and 2) when they do make a trip, Dad takes a nap before they leave so they drive at night while the kids are asleep in the car.

◊ Mom does not let Jason play with his friend John because John often encourages Jason to do things he should not.

◊ Bob and Kathy's kids usually present a problem when they are visiting friends or family, especially when other kids are there. They decided to take turns keeping a close watch on their kids. This means that one of them misses much of the adult conversations. However, it helped them to prevent much misbehavior.

6. Reinforce Opposite Behaviors

Another approach to reducing misbehavior is by using reinforcement instead of a behavior reduction technique. This idea sounds good in theory, but research has shown that this approach is not very effective when used alone. However, when it is used in conjunction with a behavior reduction strategy, it can be very helpful.

The basic idea is that you reinforce behavior that is the *opposite* of (or is incompatible with) the misbehavior you are

---

[8]Chapter 11 deals with the topic of misbehavior in public places.

trying to reduce. For example, if your children often fight over toys, then it would be important to reinforce them whenever you see them cooperating. Because fighting over toys and being cooperative are incompatible (i.e., they cannot happen at the same time), if you increase the cooperation, presumably you would be decreasing the fighting over toys. It is important to remember that reinforcing opposite behaviors should *supplement* other approaches because it probably will not work by itself.

Examples of reinforcing opposite behaviors include:

◊ Mrs. Mulcahy makes it a point to tell her son Robert that she appreciates it after he asks for things nicely (he usually asks in a rude or demanding way).

◊ Whenever her boys agree to watch a video, one mom complements them for cooperating (they usually fight over what to watch).

7. *Avoiding Accidental Reinforcement*

One important way to remove the incentive for misbehavior is fairly straightforward — try to determine the ways in which you may be accidentally reinforcing your child's misbehavior. Accidental reinforcement occurs when we give the child what he wants following a misbehavior, often without even realizing it. For example, we accidentally reinforce yelling when we scream at our children (by modeling). We accidentally reinforce a tantrum when we try to negotiate the problem to get him to stop the tantrum. We accidentally reinforce a child for arguing or whining when we give in or at least accommodate their request while they are arguing or whining.

One way to find out how we may be accidentally reinforcing misbehavior is to look back at Chapter 3 under the section called "Consistency." Inconsistency accidentally reinforces misbehavior, so as you reduce inconsistency, you reduce accidental reinforcement.

A second way to discover sources of accidental reinforcement is to analyse a typical scenario when the misbehavior occurs. You want to determine three things:

1. What happened *prior to* the incident
2. What happened *during* the incident
3. What happened *after* the incident

Here is an example of how this would work. Chad throws frequent tantrums. His parents discuss what usually happens in this situation (when Chad is not around to hear them). They conclude that *prior* to a tantrum, Chad usually either asks for something and his parents say no, or he is told he has to do something he does not want to do (e.g., a chore). *During* the tantrum, his parents yell at him or ask him what the problem is, or reason with him and try to make him see it their way. Sometimes (but not often), Chad's parents try to strike a deal with Chad to compromise on their expectation or compromise on what he asked for. *After* the tantrum, Chad has calmed down and is apparently satisfied with the compromise (in those situations when there is a compromise).

It occurs to Chad's parents that they have been accidentally reinforcing Chad to continue with the tantrums by giving him attention during the tantrum, and by occasionally compromising their position.[9] Because Chad is satisfied with the outcome, he is likely to use a tantrum to get his way on future occasions. Also, parents do not need to give in every time to reinforce the misbehavior. Even if parents occasionally give in, the child figures the misbehavior is worth a try because he might get what he wants.

A third way to determine sources accidental reinforcement is to ask other adults (spouses, your parents, your siblings, or friends) if they can see you accidentally reinforcing your child. If it is a person you trust, you may find they have a very good idea of how you are accidentally reinforcing misbehavior, but have been too polite to tell you![10] Often we are unaware of

---

[9]Under some circumstances, there is nothing wrong with parents changing their mind or making compromises. However, you should *never* do this when your is child arguing, whining, or throwing a tantrum or else he learns to get what he wants by behaving this way.

things that are obvious to others because we are in the middle of the situation. This suggestion would take a good dose of humility and openness on your part, but if someone whose judgment you trust sees you interact with your child, their suggestions may yield valuable insight.

Why Incentive Removal Works

Incentive removal works because of a principle called *learned helplessness.* Learned helplessness in the context of child discipline refers to when a child continually fails at attempts to misbehave (or fails to receive a benefit from the misbehavior), so he eventually stops trying to misbehave in that way.[11] For example, if a parent consistently used the *broken record* technique (described above) when her child argues, her child would eventually learn that he is helpless at influencing his mother through arguing. He finally stops because he constantly fails at getting his way by arguing.

Consistency is the most important key to having children feel helpless in their attempts to misbehave. If parents consistently follow through with action, kids will learn there is no room for success at misbehaving. When they realize this, they will eventually decrease (or eliminate) their attempts at the misbehavior you are working on. Awareness of the principle of learned helplessness should help parents stick with an approach

---

[10] On the other hand, it is important to be cautious about the advice of others, because it is entirely possible to get *bad* advice. Use your good judgment in evaluating any interpretations others give you.

[11] In adult clinical psychology, the term *learned helplessness* is used differently, although the underlying psychological principle is the same. It refers to the phenomenon of a person who no longer tries to pursue certain activities because they have had no success in the past. For example, a depressed person may refuse to attempt to meet new people, try new things, or generally better himself. This is because such attempts in the past either did not work, or resulted in rejection, pain, or embarrassment. Thus, repeated failures can result in a person not trying anymore. The major difference with the way the term is used in the context of child discipline is that we are focusing on becoming "helpless" regarding *misbehavior*, while the term in adult clinical psychology usually refers to people feeling helpless about positive behavior.

until they see results.

Examples of learned helplessness (using various techniques) include:

◊ Every time Sarah ignores her mom's request to stop doing something, her mom heads over to see to it that Sarah stops. Eventually, Sarah simply complies because she learns there is no way mom will back down in that type of situation (Proximity).

◊ David and Andrew have stopped roughhousing because they get an automatic 5 minutes isolation. Thus, they cannot even misbehave in this way, even if they want to! (Isolation/Nipping Misbehavior in the Bud).

◊ Kara eventually learns that tantrums are worthless because they no longer allow her to get her way (Ignoring/Time Out).

◊ Five year old Jamie used to get out of his chair when his parents punished him with isolation. He no longer does because he learned that they would stand over him, and even restrain him if necessary. He learned there was no use in trying to get off the chair during isolation (Physical Persuasion).

Using Approaches In Combination

Any time a child is experiencing a problem with behavior, improvement occurs best when strategies are applied in combination. You can use almost any combination of strategies presented in this chapter and the previous chapter. Parents can learn to think through a situation, "brainstorm" various possible ways they can influence their child to improve, and come up with a plan. The next chapter will help you put together a plan.

Examples of combining strategies:

◊ To get him to stop swearing, Jimmy's parents used a combination of *isolation* and *response cost* (he lost a quarter each time). Also when he went a day without swearing, they gave him much *praise* and *encouragement*.

◊ Jackie constantly argued and challenged her parents. They began to use the *broken record* and *time out* when she became argumentative. In addition, they made it a point to spend more positive time with Jackie, when she is not arguing.

◊ Mark's parents use *isolation* and *overcorrection* when he hits his brother or sister. Immediately following an incident, he sits in a chair. Then, he has to apologize and do one of the chores of the sibling he hit (*overcorrection*).

Willful Misbehavior vs. Carelessness

Before you select an approach or combination of approaches, it is important to decide if the behavior is willful misbehavior, or careless irresponsibility. Usually when a child spills something, breaks something, forgets something, or neglects chores, they are not misbehaving on purpose. They are being careless and irresponsible (all children are irresponsible to some degree). In cases of irresponsible behavior, strategies like *logical consequences, positive practice,* and in some cases *response cost* or *overcorrection* make the most sense. You are not trying to *punish* your child in these situations, you are trying to *teach* him to be more responsible (more careful, less forgetful, etc.). *Isolation, withdrawal of a privilege* (unless it also happens to be a logical consequence), or spanking should not be used to teach responsibility. These are all punitive in nature. However, if the child is purposefully misbehaving, then *isolation, withdrawal of privilege, response cost, overcorrection,* and *logical consequences* are all possible strategies to use.

SUMMARY

There are two ways to reduce misbehavior. One way is to make the cost of the misbehavior too high. With this approach, your goal is to discourage the misbehavior based upon negative consequences. The second way to reduce misbehavior is by removing your child's incentive for misbehaving. Your goal is to take away what is reinforcing the behavior. A variety of negative consequences and incentive removal techniques were discussed above. Parents can select, combine, and adapt from among the strategies in this chapter to effectively reduce most kinds of misbehavior. However, *the strategy you use is only one half of the picture!* It is *how* you use the strategy that is usually the most important part of effective discipline. I strongly encourage all readers to go back over the contents of Chapter 3 so that the material is so familiar that they will always be aware of what makes discipline effective.

Chapter 6

Putting Together a Plan

In this chapter, you will learn:
◊ How to develop, use, and evaluate a behavior plan.

I have had parents tell me that everything makes sense in my office, yet when they are at home, and a situation arises, they feel like they forget everything and fall apart. In this chapter you will learn how to avoid this problem. You will learn how to develop and use a behavior plan for your child, so that when a situation arises, you will know exactly what to do.

A behavior plan can be as simple as deciding to use the broken record every time your child argues. Other plans may be more involved. There are several reasons you may want to use a behavior plan. Some of those reasons include:

◊ If you have had difficulty consistently following through with attempts to change behavior, a behavior plan can help you be more consistent.

◊ If there are several behaviors you would like to change, a behavior plan can help you organize and prioritize your efforts.

◊ If your child has discipline problems in more than one setting (e.g., home, school, sitter's), a behavior plan can help provide consistency across settings.

◊ If there is more than one person who is routinely involved with the discipline of your child (e.g., two parents, a grandparent, a sitter), a behavior plan can help provide more consistency.

◊ If you want to define very clearly to yourself and your child what constitutes a misbehavior, and what the consequences will be, a behavior plan can give you the clarity you'll need.

Basically, a behavior plan can help anytime you want to know exactly what you are going to do, and how you are going to do it.

I find it interesting that professional football coaches stand on the sidelines holding a card with their plays on it. They know their plays extremely well, so it seems amazing that they would feel the need to keep such a guide handy. The reason they do this is because in the heat of the moment, they want to be sure that they can make the right decision about which play to use in a given situation. In the same way, a behavior plan can help assure you that you are going to take the right approach in a given situation. You develop a plan carefully and thoughtfully at a time when you are calm and rational. Then, in the heat of the moment, you can be more assured you will respond in a way that will produce results.

Putting together a behavior plan is actually rather simple. The information in this chapter, combined with the worksheets in the back of the book, will make the process simple.

How to develop a behavior plan

Identify the behaviors to change. The first step is to list the behaviors you wish to change. This could include misbehavior you want to reduce (e.g., "hits sister"), as well as responsible behavior you want to develop (e.g., "cleans room when asked"). Be as specific as possible. For example, parents often list for me "does not listen." What they really mean is "does not respond when asked to do something." Worksheet #1 in the back of the book provides a place to list those behaviors.

It is sometimes helpful to make a note of other information surrounding the behavior. For example, if your child throws a tantrum only at night before bed, write down "throws tantrums before bed" instead of simply "throws tantrums." Indicate what usually happens just prior to the misbehavior (e.g., when I get on the phone or someone comes to visit, he begins to . . ." or "whenever his little brother takes one of his toys, that's when he. . ."). Also write down what usually happens in the end (e.g., "I finally give in to keep the peace," or "his sister usually gets really upset after he does it"). Making notes might help you see a pattern in the child's behavior. If you notice something that almost always precedes the misbehavior, you may be able to use *prevention* or *redirection* to avoid the misbehavior (see Chapter 5). If you can determine what reinforcement the child is getting, you may be able to use one of the *incentive removal* strategies along with a *negative consequence* (Chapter 5).

Prioritize behaviors. Once you have a list of behaviors, it will be important to prioritize them. You can do this by putting a number next to each behavior on the list you have. There are two ways to prioritize your list. The first way is to arrange them according to how severe or annoying the problem is. The second way is to arrange them according to how easy it would be to correct the problem, with the easiest getting the highest priority. For example, "argues a lot" would be much easier to correct than "lies a lot."

The reason for arranging your list from easiest to hardest is because this may be a more successful way to proceed. If you begin with an easier behavior to change, it can give you more confidence when you begin to see improvement. If you start with the hardest behavior to change and do not see success, you can get very discouraged. Second, as you begin to change your child's behavior, he may begin to see you in a different light. Your child may begin to recognize your parental authority. By the time you get to the more difficult behaviors to change, it may be easier than if you had not already been successful improving other areas. If you come to two behaviors that should take about equal effort to change, you may want to go for the more bothersome one first.

One step at a time. This was discussed in Chapter 3, so you may want to go back and review there. Once you have your list of behaviors prioritized, you will select one or two of those behaviors to begin to work on.

Identify possible plans. Once you have identified the behaviors and prioritized them, you will need to identify what possible approaches you may use. Use Worksheet #2 for this. Make a list of all of the possible approaches that could be used for this misbehavior. You will not be using all of them, but you want to make yourself aware of the alternatives. Then select the approach or approaches you will use to deal with the behavior. You may want to reread the sections of the book that cover the strategies you have selected.

Communicate the plan to your child. The next step is to let your child know what you will expect.[1] You will also need to explain the consequence (good or bad) if she meets or does not meet your expectations. This should be done in a positive, constructive way, not in a way that is demeaning and insensitive to the child's self-esteem. Make sure you are very specific about what constitutes a misbehavior, or what constitutes the successful completion of a chore.

Evaluate your plans. After a plan of action has been in place for one or more weeks, you may want to monitor how it is working. It is important to consider if you have been carefully following the "keys to improving behavior" (see Chapter 3). Also consider how your child is responding. Is it time to add a greater combination of approaches? Should you keep doing what you are doing? Should you change the rewards or the consequences you are using? In many cases you will have to make changes and adjustments.

Other Things to Consider

Only use approaches you feel comfortable with. You must select an approach that you feel comfortable using. If not, you may find yourself taking a half-hearted approach and you will

---

[1] An exception to this is the *broken record* approach. This is a technique that you should use without explanation. If you explain the *broken record,* your child may try to undermine it.

not be successful. There are many suggestions in this book, and I do not expect that every reader would feel comfortable with all of them. Some approaches may take getting used to. For example, parents often feel a little awkward at first when they use the broken record technique (see Chapter 5). After they use it, they are amazed at how well it works and quickly become comfortable with it. If you like an idea but think you will feel a little awkward, give it a try. New things usually feel awkward at first.

Be positive. Do not let a behavior plan turn your home into a little boot camp. It is important to remember that you must be making ongoing efforts to develop a better relationship with your child. I am sure your goal is not simply to create an obedient little soldier. You want to develop a responsible child who is "on your side," and who is learning right from wrong. Developing a better relationship with your child will help you toward that goal.

Get your spouse involved. It is important that you get your spouse involved in both the development and use of the behavior plan. Any adult that may be involved in discipline with your child should have a part in the plan. For example, if you are a single mom, and your mother lives in the same home as you, you will probably want to get her involved.

Sometimes one parent finds it hard to get the other parent involved in a behavior plan. If this is the case, it will be necessary to convince the other person why he or she needs to be a part of the plan. You may begin by pointing out that things are rather miserable when your child misbehaves, and that the plan should help. Explain how inconsistency is a major contributor to misbehavior, and if all adults in the child's home respond in the same way, you can provide the consistency needed to improve the behavior. You may even ask your spouse to read this book, or at least Chapters 1, 2, and 3.

It will also be important that each spouse supports the efforts of the other. Otherwise, the child might play one parent against the other. Your child needs to see a united front. All adults in the home must make a team effort. Communication between adults is crucial.

Treat "back talk" as a separate misbehavior. When your child is "mouthy" or speaks to you disrespectfully, treat it as a separate misbehavior. For example, let's say you are working on Behavior #1 and #2 from your priority list, and "back talk" is not one of them. You provide consequences to your child when he does Behavior #1 or #2, and he gets mouthy when you provide those consequences. It would be better to let that slide until one or both of Behavior #1 and #2 are under control. Remember, do not worry if your child gets in the "last word." You make sure you follow through with action. Then, you can deal with the back talk when you reach that point on your priority list.

SUMMARY

Good discipline starts with good planning. You are more equipped to deal with your child's misbehavior when you have a plan. When the misbehavior occurs, you will be able to respond automatically, immediately, and consistently. It is this kind of responding from parents that will change behavior.

Chapter 7

When Nothing Seems To Work

Some of the techniques described in Chapters 3 through 5 will seem familiar to many parents. Actually, none of those techniques are new. They have all been the subject of research over the years, and have been shown to be effective if applied properly in the right situations. There are several reasons why parents use such approaches and still have difficulties with their children. I encourage you to go back and read Chapter 3 again. This will remind you of the important elements needed to effectively use any technique. Below are reasons why these techniques might not work, based on some of the concepts from Chapter 3.

Usually, when behavioral strategies are used with children and do not seem to work, there is nothing wrong with the actual technique. Rather, it does not work because of one or more of the following issues.

1. The technique is not being used consistently

Consistency is the most important element in any attempt to change behavior. Significant lapses in consistency can spoil most attempts to improve behavior. Are you giving warnings? Are you relying on explanations or yelling instead of taking immediate action? Does your discipline change with your mood? Any of these can cause a good technique to fail.

2. The plan is given up too soon

When using a plan, the behavior often gets worse first. Some parents quit before the plan had time to show improvement. Also, parents may abandon a plan too soon because they see immediate results. Sometimes, it takes weeks of consistently applied strategies before parents see a breakthrough. Therefore, it may be wiser to keep a potentially effective plan in place until it is clear that the acceptable behavior has become a habit.

3. Not enough is being done

I have mentioned several times the importance of combining influences to improve behavior. Too often, parents try one suggestion and get frustrated when it fails. Usually, kids need more than one simple little trick. I often hear parents say "nothing works with her, we've tried everything." Many parents try one idea after another, with each approach failing just like the previous one. The solution is 1) try more than one strategy at the same time and 2) stick with your plan longer. You probably have not given it sufficient time to take effect.

4. Your child is not making the connection

Your child may miss the connection between behavior and consequence for many reasons:

Expectations not clear. If the demands are not clearly explained ahead of time, your child may not make the proper connections. The same is the case if a child is not clearly told why he is getting the reinforcement or consequences.

Too many demands. If your child is suddenly bombarded with many demands, she can get very confused. She will not be able to make connections between behaviors and consequences.

Inconsistency. Inconsistency in the form of multiple warnings, threats, and second chances, make it hard for children to learn what we are trying to teach them.

Poor timing. With poor or inconsistent timing of reinforcement or consequences, your child may not learn what you expect.

Discipline based upon mood. If discipline is based on your mood, your child thinks he is being punished because of your mood rather than for his misbehavior. Therefore, he does not make the proper connections. Calm discipline is most effective.

5. *The wrong technique is being used*

Different situations need different types of approaches. For example, using ignoring when a child is not misbehaving to get your attention can make things worse, not better. Trying to use positive reinforcement (by itself) to reduce *misbehavior* usually will not work. Think carefully about which approach fits the situation, and has a good chance to succeed. You should be guided by your knowledge of the information in this book combined with good common sense and your familiarity with your child.

6. *Did not use a plan or did not stick with a plan*

Parents who take a haphazard approach, without a consistent plan to follow, will be less likely to see improvement. A clear plan helps parents with confidence and consistency.

A Note about Hyperactivity and Emotionally Troubled Children

Hyperactivity and attention deficits. At least half of the parents I have worked with have children with difficulties in this area. Children who are hyperactive, impulsive, and have attention problems need the kind of firm limits discussed in this book more than anyone. Parents of such children will have a tougher job, however. *These children need much more consistency and more immediate consequences than a typical child.* Often, it takes longer for them to learn limits, even though their intelligence may be average or better. I would strongly recommend that you consult with both your child's physician and a school psychologist from your child's school district.[1] They have ways to help. Also, one small company has gathered together a wide variety of materials on Attention Deficits and Hyperactivity into one catalog. It's called A.D.D. Warehouse

---

[1] Consultation with your district's school psychologist would be free of charge.

and you can receive their catalog by calling (800) ADD-WARE.

Emotionally troubled children. If you have a child with emotional problems, you can still make a positive impact on him. However, I would not recommend you do this without the support of a psychologist or other professional. You may want to take this book along and show the counselor what you have been learning. Then, the counselor can help customize an approach for you because he or she would know your situation.

In the meantime, you may want to find out if your child is a good candidate for counseling. The combination of counseling for your child and your improved discipline and helping skills may be what is needed to get results. Please remember that this book is not designed to usurp the role of professional assistance. There is much you can gain from interacting with a psychologist or counselor that you could not get from a book.

Hundreds of research studies have been done on children and their behavior. Research has shown that no matter how severe a child's behavior problems may be, no matter how severe an emotional or psychological problem he may have, positive change is possible. Certainly some children take more effort, and make less progress, but *any child can improve.* By properly using the techniques and principles presented in this book, you can begin to see an improvement in your child. Right now, the next step is up to you!

Chapter 8

Building Self-Esteem

Self-esteem can have an important impact on a child's behavior. A child who is discouraged and has a low self-esteem may decide, "why not misbehave, I'm a bad kid anyway?" A child with good self-esteem feels more secure and may be more willing to cooperate.

We parents play a significant role in the development of our children's self-esteem. Whether we know it or not, we are constantly sending our child messages about herself. If we do not have much time to spend with her, she may get the message, "I'm not important." If we spend much time in positive activities, she may get the message, "I'm important and my parents care for me." If we are always yelling and hostile, she may get the message, "I'm a bad kid," or "they don't love me."

A difficulty arises when your child frequently misbehaves. You spend so much time correcting his behavior. He gets very few positive messages from parents or teachers. There are two solutions to this difficulty. First, when you correct your child, it should be done in a calm, controlled fashion. This was covered in previous chapters. A hostile approach (anger, yelling) adds nothing constructive to discipline. Rather, it can slowly destroy a child by sending negative messages. These messages attack the child as a person, and do not deal with the misbehavior.

The second solution to dealing with the frequently misbehaving child is to take a positive approach. A positive approach includes the following:

Finding ways to praise. A parent can vigilantly watch for good behavior to reinforce. Too often we concentrate on bad behavior and do not recognize some of the many little positive things we could reinforce. Some have suggested giving your child two positive comments for every one correcting comment.

Be a source of encouragement. You can be a positive source of encouragement for your child, whatever her interests or responsibilities happen to be. Whether it is positively affirming her for the dance lessons, or helping her with her homework, you send a strong positive message that you are interested in what she is doing.

Initiating positive interactions or activities. When you take initiative and get involved in positive activities with your child, this sends him the message that you appreciate his company and that he is important to you. Parents get frustrated when such efforts seem to "fail" because the child seems to take advantage, act up, or generally make the parent angry. However, you will see positive results in the long run if you persist in doing things together with your child. (Sometimes, discipline may be necessary even when you are involved in a fun activity. For example: "Kevin, if you are not going to play by the rules, we will have to put the game away").

If your child gets more positive messages from you, and is no longer treated in a hostile manner when he misbehaves, he will begin to feel more encouraged to cooperate with you. The more positive time you spend with your child, the less time you will spend in confrontation and discipline.

Tips for developing self-esteem and self-confidence

Avoid name calling — address the behavior, not the person. All too often when a child misbehaves, his parent will attack him as a person instead of dealing with his behavior. Consider the following two statements:

1) "You're such a slob."

2) "Sean, please pick up after yourself. You cannot go outside to play until you clean up these toys."

The first statement attacks the child and does not address the behavior. The second statement clearly communicates an expectation with no negative messages attached. If you make sweeping statements about your child (such as "you're lazy," "you're such a pain," "you're acting like a 2 year old," "stop being a jerk,") you send him a discouraging message about himself that will not help change his behavior. Consider the following:

1) "You're such a naughty boy"
2) "That was a naughty thing to do"

The first statement sends a message that *he* is naughty, and you disapprove of *him*. The second one tells the child that what he *did* was wrong; you disapprove of the *behavior*. There is a very different message sent to a child when we use name calling than when we focus on correcting the behavior.

Why do parents routinely say things to their children that attack them but do not help the behavior? Probably to release frustration. When frustrated, parents sometimes do not think about their child's best interests. Also, this frustration results from not knowing what to do when children misbehave. The principles in this book will help minimize that problem. Instead of relying on anger and hostility, you can now use a variety of strategies and principles to help correct misbehavior and boost good behavior. *There should be no reason to rely on negative statements to try to control your children.* Action, not hostile words, will change behavior and protect self-esteem.

Avoid the terms "always" and "never." When you make statements like, "you never do what I tell you," or "you always make me mad," your child can begin to take such comments to heart. They can easily take it as a direct attack on them because they feel you are hounding them about a personality flaw. A more reasonable way to say it would be, "I do not like it when you . . ." This helps you and your child focus on the behavior instead of attacking them with a history lesson about what they have or haven't done in the past.

Watch your tone of voice. We can communicate a message

by how we say something. If we say in a polite or neutral tone of voice, "Alex, could you please clean your room now, you can watch TV after you're done," we clearly communicate our expectations. If we say the same thing in a sing-song nagging intonation, we put a power challenge to our child that does not need to be part of the request. Our tone of voice says, "Here you go again, watching TV before your room is clean; you're so irresponsible." Your literal words may not say it, but your tone of voice may.

Avoid comparing children. No two children are the same. There is usually no benefit to making remarks like, "why can't you behave like your brother?" If you use one child as the standard for another, you can frustrate and demean the child who does not "measure up." In addition, you may promote sibling resentment.

Avoid perfectionism. An easy way to destroy your child's self-esteem is to be a perfectionist and always expect more from him than he can reasonably give at the present time. It is very discouraging to never be able to please your parents because what you do is never good enough. I was working with one mother who knew she was a perfectionist, but made no apologies about it. She said she frequently praised and complimented her son. However, further discussion revealed she rarely gave him a genuine compliment — there was always a "but" attached. For example, she would say, "Nice job cleaning your room, but your bed spread is very wrinkled." "Thank you for setting the table, but the forks go on the left side." When a parent compliments this way, the child learns that any praise or encouragement is not genuine. When they hear a compliment, they know there is a correction that will soon follow.

An effective way to avoid the perfectionism approach is to allow the child to occasionally rest on his laurels for a while. If you expect constant, ongoing improvement, you are dangling a carrot in front of your child, and he will never feel he has accomplished anything. If your expectations allow for a time where improvement levels off for awhile, your child can relax for a time and feel good about the progress he has made thus far.

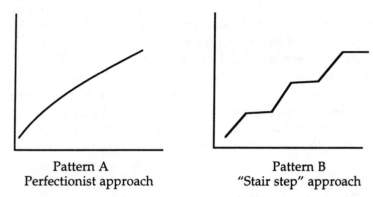

Pattern A
Perfectionist approach

Pattern B
"Stair step" approach

With the perfectionism pattern (pattern A), the child is always expected to do more. He gets very discouraged because he never feels like he has accomplished anything. He does not think his parents appreciate his progress because they are always asking for more. It is a constant, uphill battle. With the *stair step approach* (pattern B), the child is also expected to make progress, but he is allowed a time to "rest." At these times, he can relax and feel a sense of accomplishment. He knows his parents appreciate his progress because they really praise and encourage him, even when he is at a leveling off place in his progress.

Another way to deal with parental perfectionism is the "one step at a time" principle (see Chapter 3). If you must correct a child's behavior to meet your standards, only work on one thing at a time. Wait until your child has mastered this before working on something else. Constant correction about many different behaviors can be very frustrating and discouraging to a child. The end result of such parental "nagging" is usually the opposite of what you want. To the perfectionist parent I have this advice: Give your child a break.

Children of all ages deserve dignity and respect. A child is no less human or no less of a person than an adult. Therefore, they deserve all of the dignity and respect that any adult would get. *Children should be recognized as our equals in terms of dignity and respect, even if they are not our equals in terms of wisdom, knowledge, and ability to function independently.* Therefore, we should treat our children with the utmost consideration, and not brush them aside as second class humans. Think of how quickly we consider what we do as important and what our children do as unimportant. Kids pick up on this. We speak with our children disrespectfully — in ways we would never speak to another adult. Just because we must provide leadership and authority for our children does not mean that our responsibility should be carried out without recognizing the inherent dignity that each youngster has.

Throughout this handbook, there have been several references to providing discipline without yelling and hostility. This is because yelling and hostility are not only ineffective they also can damage self-esteem. The hostile approach is also a disrespectful way to treat anyone, let alone someone we love. I do not write these words to make parents feel guilty. I write to challenge parents to use some of the many approaches described in this book. Then they can eliminate the anger and hostility that can often accompany attempts at discipline.

Our time — our children's most valuable asset Someone once said that children spell love T-I-M-E. There is no better way of showing a child that you care about her than by spending time with her. This means "quantity time" as well as "quality time." Praise, encouragement, fun activities, and other positive experiences build up a child to make her feel loved. This is the type of relationship you want to build and should be the context of your discipline. Both research and common wisdom have shown that clear, firm limits in the context of a warm, loving relationship will result in the most successful discipline.

Chapter 9

Solutions to Common Discipline Problems

In this chapter, strategies you learned from this book will be applied to common problems. This is not an complete list, but only several examples. You must be familiar with Chapters 1-5 to use the information presented below. To find the description of a strategy mentioned below, look back in Chapters 3 through 5 for a "refresher."

Arguing

Broken record. There are three effective ways to deal with arguing, all described in Chapter 5 under "Incentive Removal." The most helpful approach is the broken record (see Chapter 5).

Time out. When your child begins to argue, you tell her that she will go to her room if she continues to argue. For this to work, you must *immediately* send her to her room when she begins arguing, with no additional warnings. She only needs to be there a few minutes, and you must be ready to keep sending her back for a few more minutes for *each time* she attempts to argue. If this is done every time, you will see improvement.

Planned ignoring. If your child argues, you can tell him, "We're done with that discussion, and there's no reason to say anything more. If you continue to bring it up, I am not going to even listen. If you want to talk about something else, I'll be glad to talk." Then go about your business. Turn a deaf ear to your child if he continues to argue. When he realizes that he has no argument, he eventually stops. If he keeps trying to argue, you may break your silence with, "we are not talking about that." Also, you can tell him that if he continues to argue, he will have to sit in his room for 5 minutes (*time out* can be a back up to the broken record and planned ignoring).

Back talk/mouthiness

Isolation. If you put your child in a chair for 5 minutes *every time* he talks back, the back talk will decrease.

Positive practice. Your child would be required to repeat what he wanted to say in a respectful manner, two or three times. If done consistently he will begin to think twice about talking back, if he knows he will have to say it three times.

Response Cost. Each time he talks back, he loses a coin or token or whatever you are using for your response-cost system.

Limit television watching. The average evening of prime-time television gives children a lesson in how to talk disrespect-fully to their parents. TV sitcoms portray children who are mouthy and "smarter" than their parents. Research on model-ing suggests that this type of program teaches disrespect.

Withdrawal of privilege. If your child is doing something he enjoys, you may tell him he has to stop doing it for awhile because of his back talk. This must be done in a calm way:

Mom: I'm sorry you spoke to me that way. We can't continue working on this model until later when you can be polite.

Child: But Mom, I've just gotta finish this, I won't do it again.

Mom: I said we can try again later (leaves room).

Whining, pestering

Time out, planned ignoring, and the *broken record,* all work with whining. Also, if you are doing something with your child, withdrawing your presence would be a *logical con-sequence.* "I'm not going to be able to help you because you're whining. We'll try later." One possibility is to say, "I'm sorry, I can't do what you asked because you whined. Maybe next time you'll ask without whining." If they automatically *do not* get what they want when they whine, whining will decrease.

Tantrums

Time out is the best approach for dealing with tantrums. *Planned ignoring* can also be used. You must be willing to let your child "cry it out" in another room, no matter how loud it gets or how long it takes. If you give in or negotiate, you will teach him he can get what he wants by throwing a tantrum.

Neglectful of chores

Positive reinforcement. Positive incentives are the most preferred motivator. *Verbal praise* and *encouragement, activity reinforcement,* and *token* or *material reinforcers* can all be used to help motivate your child to do something she is not particularly interested in doing.

First Things First. If positive incentives are not enough, you may want to use the *first things first* principle. This should be your first line of attack against neglect of chores. If you use this consistently (i.e., use it every time and see it through every time), you can eliminate this problem most of the time.

Positive Practice. If your child consistently forgets, you could use positive practice. If he does not complete the chore by a certain time (which you agreed upon in advance), he may have to do it three times.

Overcorrection. If your child does not complete a chore by a time you agreed upon, he will have to do it along with another related chore that he was not originally expected to do.

Hot seat. If your child flatly refuses to do his chore, the *hot seat* may be helpful. Remember, this should only be used in situations when 1) your child is being defiant and 2) he has to do something he can easily do, but is refusing due to a power struggle, 3) you have the time to see it through (not before bed or when you may be leaving to go somewhere).

Response-Cost. Each time he neglects his daily chore, he loses one item from your response-cost system.

Often we parents do not see to it that our children follow

through on their chores. We must be willing to remind, reinforce, and follow through until it becomes a habit for them. Only then should we use things like *overcorrection* or *positive practice* as a consequence for not doing chores.

Watches too much TV/plays video games too much

The most obvious way is also the best way: put structured limits on these activities. Once their time limit is up for the day, follow through and make sure they stop the activity.

Withdrawal of privilege. If your child puts up resistance about stopping at the agreed time, inform him (calmly and respectfully — as always) that he will not be able to watch TV (or play video games) the following day (or block of time).

Sloppiness/not picking up after themselves

Clearly stated expectations. We need to be willing to tell our children and then *remind* them to take care of their responsibilities. Expecting them to do everything without reminders is unrealistic.

Praise/Encouragement. Any time you "catch" your child picking up after herself, tell her how much you appreciate it. Review the types of praise described in Chapter 4.

Positive practice. When you see your child's things laying around, have her practice putting them away a few times.

First Things First. She pick's up after herself before she is allowed to do anything else.

Overcorrection. Your child may have to clean up more than her own things if, over time, she does not respond to a consistent dose of the *first things first* principle or *positive practice.*

Fighting with siblings

Isolation and time out. These are the best approaches to use with fighting. Keep in mind what parent #2 did in Chapter 3 (under "Less is More").

Withdrawal of privilege. Your children will not be allowed to continue the activity they were doing when they started fighting. This privilege would be withdrawn for the rest of the day (or for a specified block of time).

Response-Cost. A response-cost system could be set up with each of the children who participate in sibling fighting and arguing. One item is removed each time there is an incident.

If your can determine with certainty that one child is clearly the aggressor and the other is the victim, obviously you would only punish the aggressor. However, if it is unclear who did what, both should experience a consequence. This does not always result in equal justice. However, there is no such thing as equal justice in all circumstances — you just try your best. Even though the less guilty one will receive the same consequence as the more guilty, he may learn to avoid involvement in fighting situations in the future.

Not listening or complying

Proximity. When your child does not respond to your requests, it will be important to *immediately* approach him, stand over him, and see to it that he follows through.

No warnings. When you ask him to do something, give a reasonable amount of time, then follow through with action if he does not comply. Do not warn, threaten, or plead. Remember, actions speak louder than words.

If you ask your child not to do something, and he runs right out and does it as if he didn't hear you (i.e., not maliciously), then an appropriate logical consequence related to the misbehavior would be appropriate (or use *positive practice* or *overcorrection*). Also 5 minute *isolation* may be appropriate if no logical consequence can be found.

Problems at school, on the bus, or at the day care

Parents must realize that the teacher is the person primarily responsible for managing children at school. Short of attending school with them, parents have no direct opportunities to influence their children while they are at school. Teachers are in the position to enforce immediate and consistent limits. However, parents can play a supportive role in following through at home with an approach a teacher is using at school. A simple home-school checklist that is developed specifically for your child can be used to help you monitor school behavior. You can follow through at home with rewards and consequences based upon your child's checklist. A checklist could look like this:

___ Remains in seat
___ Keeps hands and feet to himself
___ Finishes his work on time

The teacher assigns a 0, 1, or 2 to each of the blanks. The child receives some reward at home for a good overall score, a withdrawal of a privilege for a poor score, and a pep talk for an in-between score. Teachers are often willing to do this sort checklist because it only takes 20 to 30 seconds at the end of each day. The list is sent home with the child in a sealed envelope each day. If no envelope shows up, a call to the teacher is in order (some kids will intercept poor checklists). Each child's checklist is custom made and a stack of copies are provided to the teacher. Additional ideas for home-school behavior management strategies could be generated in consultation with the school psychologist from your school district.

Teachers, bus drivers, and baby sitters may need to know from you what works with your child and what does not. However, things that work at home may not work at school. Teachers have many more children to attend to than you do. However, ongoing communication with other adults who deal with your child is important. Try to create an atmosphere of cooperation between yourself, the teacher, bus driver, etc. Avoid blaming those adults when your child misbehaves while your child is their responsibility.

Disruptive during meals

Logical consequences. If your child is frequently disruptive during meals, you can avoid many confrontations by nipping the behavior in the bud. When he disrupts, tell him he will have to eat in a different location so he will not ruin everyone else's meal. Make sure it is an undesirable place — not in front of the TV in the living room! Do not send your child to a humiliating place like a closet or in the garage on a cold day. The point is that the child cannot handle himself while eating with the family, so he will have to eat that meal elsewhere.

Response-Cost. With each incidence of disruption, an item is removed from a response-cost system.

Not eating a meal then asking for food later

Logical consequences. When a child is "not hungry" and does not eat the family meal, wrap it up, put it in the refrigerator. You then microwave it later when she says she's hungry. Do not get in the habit of giving her interesting things to eat later in the evening because she was not interested in supper. Your child must learn that she will not receive any dessert or other food to eat until the original meal (or some agreed upon portion of it) has been eaten.

Prevention. Make sure your child does not snack between meals. Also, make sure that your child starts off with small portions of new foods, in case she does not like it. Do not force your child to eat something she does not like and has genuinely tried. It is important to encourage kids to try new foods, but do not force feed a child when she does not like something. This can create more problems than it solves.

Lying

Lying is one of the most difficult behaviors to deal with effectively. It is very easy to accidentally reinforce lying by the way we punish. Lying cannot be dealt with using some simple strategy. To adequately deal with lying, you will need to use *several* at the same time.

Modeling. The first step in dealing with lying is to make absolutely certain that you and your spouse do not lie — not even little white lies or exaggerations. Children learn that untruthfulness or dishonesty is okay because they hear their parents doing it. *All the lectures in the world will not help a child who knows his parents lie or stretch the truth.* As parents, we must learn to model truthfulness, even when it makes things inconvenient for us. What a powerful point we can make to our children if we can say, "your dad and I always tell the truth, and we expect that you will always tell the truth."

Limit television viewing. Television is a training school for lying and general dishonesty. Just carefully watch an evening of "family" sitcoms. You will be amazed at the constant barrage of lies and misrepresentations that characters use to get themselves out of awkward situations (usually accompanied by a laugh track). Why let your child see this? Limiting television can help limit your child's exposure to negative role models.

Clearly state your expectations. It is important that you clearly explain to your child what is truth and what is a lie. As children get older, lies become more subtle. It is important that children know why honesty and trust are so important. Lecturing your child will not make much difference. But instructing your child in the importance of truthfulness may help him when combined with other approaches to deal with lying.

Positive Reinforcement. It is important to not take truthfulness for granted. We must reinforce our children when they tell the truth. When you are certain your child has told the truth you should reinforce her for it. This is especially the case when she may have had a benefit to lying but chooses not to. Any of the types of reinforcement described in Chapter 4 can be used.

Negative Consequences. If you have caught your child in a clear lie, you should provide a consequence for it. Ideally, it should be logically related to the situation that prompted the lying. If not, you may need to select another consequence from

Chapter 5. If you are not sure whether or not your child is lying, you should *not* provide a consequence. If you punish your child when he has told the truth, he may think it doesn't matter if he lies or not — he still gets the same punishment.

Natural consequences. We should not cover up for our child's lying. If he has lied to a teacher, for example, we should expect that he experience the consequences that naturally result from it. When we cover up for our child, we promote lying.

Response-Cost. Whenever you can determine that your child has lied, he loses an item from the response-cost system.

Prevention. Do not put your child in a situation that encourages lying. For example, if you hear a crash in the next room, do not run in, look at the damage and angrily say, "Did you do this?" Children lie to avoid consequences. It would be better to simply administer a consequence if appropriate (assuming it is clear what happened and you do not need your child's explanation) rather than encourage him to lie to keep from incriminating himself.

Incentive Removal. A lie is almost always a bigger problem than the misbehavior a child is lying about. In cases like this, you may want to waive any consequence for the other misbehavior in exchange for the truth. This works best in situations where you can be fairly certain you are getting the truth (i.e., where you can piece things together by other means). A child will learn to tell the truth when he feels secure that telling the truth will not result in negative consequences.

In more difficult cases of lying, you may need to use more drastic strategies. One involves carefully monitoring and checking up on your child. She must know that she can't be trusted and she can only be believed if her story can be verified by other means. Some would argue that this would not result in very good parent-child relations. Actually, the lying already damaged the parent-child relations, and verifying everything is a first step toward rebuilding trust. As verification results in more instances of truthful behavior, checking up slowly fades away and trust is rebuilt. This verification approach is a form of natural consequence (i.e., a natural consequence to lying is that people will not trust you).

Another drastic approach would be to "trap" your child in a lie. This would involve inquiring of your child about a certain circumstance that you already know about. If he tells the truth, you can reinforce him for it. If he lies, you provide a consequence. This may seem sneaky to some, but it is a drastic response that could be used when lying becomes a habit.

If these suggestions are carefully followed in combination with one another, you should see a reduction in lying. If you see no progress despite carefully following these suggestions, you may want to seek professional help for the problem.

Creating your own solutions

Using the common problems in this chapter as examples, you can create your own solutions to a wide variety of discipline problems. Go through Chapter 6, "Putting Together A Plan," and use Worksheet 2 in the back of the book to write down possible intervention plans. The solutions provided in this chapter give you several examples of what you could come up with by putting together your own plan based upon the ideas presented in this book.

Chapter 10

Misbehavior in Public Situations

Dealing with misbehavior in public can be very frustrating. Parents feel embarrassed and sometimes humiliated. Because it is such an important aspect of discipline, an entire chapter is devoted to it. No new information will be included in what follows. Instead, the information you have already learned will be applied to the issue of public misbehavior.

Please Note: Because this chapter relies entirely on information presented earlier in the book, it will be necessary that you read the entire contents of the book before you can make use of this chapter. Short cuts won't help.

There are a variety of public situations where discipline can present a real challenge. These could include a shopping mall, church, visiting friends, or eating at a restaurant. Before we apply the various behavioral principles to public misbehavior, there are three important things that provide the foundation for everything which follows. They are 1) providing *consistency* across situations (both at home and in public), 2) developing a *plan* to deal with a problem, and 3) learning how to *prevent* problems from occurring in the first place.

Consistency across situations. Children become a problem in public situations because they figure out that you are less likely to take action out in public. Therefore, the most important principle of effective discipline in public places is that you be *as consistent in public as you are at home.* It is important to avoid threats and warnings. There is a big temptation to try to bluff your child into good behavior by using threats. Don't say "If you can't do what I ask, we're going right home!" unless you absolutely plan on doing it without further threats or warnings. Also, because you probably feel awkward or embarrassed about using discipline in public, you can easily fall into the warning trap, which promotes misbehavior.

Develop a plan. It wouldn't make sense for a football coach to send his team on the field without a play or plan. For the same reason, it *does* makes sense for you to have a plan before taking your child to the grocery store or to grandma's house. Your plan should include both positive incentives and negative consequences. Then you will need to clearly communicate your plan to your child and follow through with action when necessary.

Prevention. Sometimes it is better to try to prevent a problem from occurring in the first place. This may mean avoiding unnecessary outings and keeping outings brief. Sometimes we parents create the problem by putting our kids in public situations where boredom prevails and they feel compelled to amuse themselves by misbehaving. For example, if you are a person who likes to go shopping, you are looking for trouble. Your children will quickly lose interest as you go from store to store looking through every clothing rack for just the right bargain while your poor child is asked to wait patiently and behave. Remember, *avoid unnecessary outings and keep outings brief.* More specific ideas will be given about prevention below.

Effective Discipline in Public

Just like at home, in public situations you should clearly state your expectations and follow through with action. Once you have developed a plan, you will need to clearly explain it to your child. You may want to explain your plan before you leave your house *and* before you enter the door to the place where you are going. Keep your comments brief. Make sure both incentives and consequences are clearly spelled out.

Keys to Improving Behavior

Consistency. Consistency is the most important element in dealing with misbehavior. Children may think that being out in public provides them with a safe haven from parental discipline. They have come to believe this because they see how reluctant we are to follow through with action when others are around. But if you take quick and confident action out in public, your child will learn that she will not be allowed to misbehave. Also, as you increase the amount of reinforcement your child receives for good behavior, she will become more motivated toward better behavior in the future. *It cannot be stressed enough that you must avoid threats, warnings, and extra chances.* These are the most common forms of inconsistency.

Timing. When you develop a plan, you will need to be sure it involves immediate consequences for your child while out in public. We often use ineffective strategies that involve a remote time in the future (e.g., "that's it, this is the last time I'm going to take you here"). Consequences that are so far off in the future will not help now, nor will they be remembered for the next time. If you must use something that is not immediate (such as withdrawing a privilege when you return home), you should use a response-cost approach so that your child experiences an immediate consequence while in that public situation.

Proximity. If you notice your child misbehaving, you will need to use the same rules of proximity that you would use at home (i.e., immediately get out of you chair and attend to the situation), despite the fact that other adults and children may be watching. I think most onlookers have more respect for parents who discipline effectively while in public than for parents who sit there and let their children misbehave.

Control your emotions. Throughout this book, the many advantages of practicing discipline without anger and hostility have been emphasized. An additional advantage is that if you keep your anger in check while in public, you decrease the chances of creating a "scene." Calm, controlled discipline works better than discipline based upon anger and changing moods.

Don't give up too soon. We were once at a fast food restaurant which had a very impressive indoor play area. The rules stated "No Jumping In The Ball Pit." We explained this to our children, but my 3 year old jumped into the ball pit anyway. I immediately had him sit next to me in the eating area. He sat on the edge of his seat eagerly watching his brothers playing. After three minutes, I told him he could go and play, and insisted that he could not jump into the ball pit. Within 30 seconds, he jumped into the ball pit again. At this point, I think most parents would conclude that having him sit out did not work. But being familiar with the principles in this book, I was not deterred. I immediately escorted him back to the eating area for another few minutes. This time, when he went back to the play area, he did not jump in the ball pit the rest of the time we were there. Lucky for me, it only took two times. However, I was prepared to repeat the procedure twenty times if I had to.

If we select a strategy to deal with misbehavior in public, we must be willing to stick with it instead of giving up if success is not immediate. When we are in public, we want immediate results to avoid embarrassment for ourselves. But we must keep in mind that we have to *train* our children by helping them to make a connection between behavior and consequence. This may take several times before we see success.

How to Increase Good Behavior

Praise and encouragement. There are many ways you can use reinforcement to promote good behavior in public. The easiest and most important is verbal reinforcement. When you catch them being good in public, tell them you appreciate it!

Activity reinforcers. You can use activity reinforcers such as a trip to a favorite restaurant or ice cream parlor at the end of the outing (such as during a trip to a mall).

Material reinforcers. Giving a treat at the check-out counter for good behavior can be an effective way to improve behavior. Some parents do not like this idea. If you use this, you can phase it out when the child becomes manageable in the store.

Token reinforcers. Children can earn tokens for good behavior in public which can be exchanged for activity or material reinforcers. Using the *mystery activity* (Chapter 4) or mystery gift (usually a small toy or treat) may keep your child eager to cooperate. Also small edible treats can be helpful, as long as they are reserved for good public behavior.

Practice. You can "rehearse" proper behavior using role playing. Behaviors that you could practice with your child may range from social etiquette (saying "please" and "thank you" at grandma's house) to sharing toys or avoiding a fight when another child starts trouble. Make a list of behaviors you are concerned about, then use role playing to have your child learn proper responses to likely situations.

With a little creativity you can go back through the other kinds of reinforcement mentioned in Chapter 4 and use them in your plan to reinforce good behavior in public.

How to Reduce Misbehavior

Negative consequences

Logical consequences. One logical consequence would be to tell your child that if she doesn't behave while out in public (make sure you mention specific expectations), she will have to leave. This would only be a meaningful consequence if your child really wants to be at that particular place. If she doesn't want to be there in the first place, this approach may have the opposite effect (i.e., it may reinforce the misbehavior). If you use this logical consequence, you must be prepared to leave at any moment and politely tell others that you have to follow through on an agreement you made with your child. Too often parents warn and warn that they are going to leave if misbehavior continues. Children see through this kind of bluff.

Less severe logical consequences can be used depending on the situation. Toys can be removed for not playing appropriately with them. A younger child may be asked to hold your hand in the store because he keeps wandering around. As situations arise ask yourself, "what consequence can I use that logically relates to this situation and does not humiliate my child in public?" Mild logical consequences can be your most effective tool to reducing misbehavior in public, as long as you can find one that is appropriate for the situation.

Isolation. Isolation can be used at other peoples' homes when you are out visiting. You may use a quiet room, a chair in a hallway, or stairs. You could avoid the warning trap and threats, by nipping misbehavior in the bud. If you give your child isolation immediately, he will learn that you will not allow misbehavior in public.

Incentive Removal

Prevention. A different approach is to prevent difficulties from occurring in the first place. This could involve not taking your child to the grocery store because you know that serious problems occur there. Then, when you have made progress with discipline at home you can begin to take your child on brief outings, and reinforce any positive behavior and provide consequences for misbehavior.

Prevention could mean that you are going to keep a higher level of *supervision* than you ordinarily would. Part of the problem is that in social situations, we often get too caught up in a conversation and we forget to keep close track of our children. So, for example, when visiting friends, you may want to have you or your spouse assigned to keep very close watch over your child while you are there. This way you can avoid many incidences of misbehavior before they have a chance to occur. Doing this may result in less adult socialization for the parent who is doing the monitoring, but you will have the assurance that your child will behave. (Remember gentleman, this is your child too — make sure you take your turn.) Over time, you can *gradually* decrease the level of supervision as your child demonstrates more responsible behavior.

Prevention could also mean that you avoid unnecessary outings and keep outings brief, especially those that are boring for your child. This was already discussed at the beginning of the chapter.

Another way to use prevention would be to *go prepared with activities* to keep your child occupied. For example, you may want to bring coloring books or quiet games to church or when you think you might be in a waiting room for awhile. This is also true for car trips. Keeping children occupied with games or activities makes more sense than spending your time screaming at them. A hand held computer game could be useful for car trips, especially if one game is reserved for trips.

Broken Record. Whining in a store should be dealt with by using the broken record technique. Children learn that we are more quick to give in while out in public because we want to "avoid a scene." If you use the broken record, your child will learn that you are not going to give in to the whining in public.

Ignoring and Time Out. Tantrums should be met with ignoring or time out. In a store, you may need to wait out the tantrum and firmly tell your child you need to get on with your business. You may want to walk ahead of your child to let him know you are *not* going to stand over him and beg and plead with him. I do not recommend the common practice I hear from parents of telling the child you are going to leave him there. Although this bluff may work, if it does not, you are stuck. Your child will learn it is a bluff (competent parents obviously cannot *really* leave their child in the mall!).

Putting together a plan

A careful review of Chapter 6 will help you put together a behavior plan. As I mentioned at the beginning of this chapter, having a plan is one of the three most important ingredients in practicing effective discipline in public situations. Having a plan can help you feel more confident about taking action in public when necessary.

Other things to consider

Resist the armchair experts. Well meaning family members, friends, or others may deter you from using good discipline. In order to avoid an awkward or embarrassing situation, they may try to convince you not to take action. "Oh Kathy, he's okay, just let him play," "it's no problem, really," "don't come down on him so hard, he's okay." In situations like this it is important to let the other person know this *is* a problem for your child and that he needs to learn to behave properly in public. Sometimes we need to evaluate the advice of others because sometimes they are right. But if you have a fair and reasonable plan in place, don't let others deter you from it simply to save the situation from temporary awkwardness. They are not the ones who will have to deal with your child on a daily basis after the incident of poor discipline is over.

Never humiliate. There is never a benefit in humiliating your child in public (or private for that matter). If you need to reprimand your child or use time out in a public setting, take your child aside and do it quietly whenever possible. There should be no reason for *you* to be the one creating a scene.

Summary

You *can* practice effective discipline in public places. It may take more thought, planning, and even creativity, but you are capable of teaching your child good behavior in public. If you can learn to maintain a high level of consistency, develop a plan of action, and learn ways to prevent problems from occurring, you can be assured of better behavior from your child.

How to Develop
a Behavior Plan

1. Identify which behaviors to deal with. (Worksheet 1)

Make a list of the behaviors you are concerned about. Then prioritize the list. Select the one or two behaviors you want to work on first.

2. Identify possible plans (Worksheet 2)

On a piece of paper, jot down possible strategies under each category listed in Worksheet #2. Only list those strategies that apply to the problem. Include more ideas than you would actually use. This is a brainstorming phase. You will select your plan from these strategies.

3. Establish the specific action you will take.

After listing the possibilities, select the strategies you think will have the greatest level of success (from the list you made using Worksheet #2). This is where you narrow your choices to make an actual plan.

4. Clearly communicate your expectations to your child.

Explain the rewards or consequences for the particular behaviors.

5. Follow through consistently with the plan.

Nip misbehavior in the bud. Avoid the warning trap, idle threats, and the other ways of compromising consistency.

6. Evaluate effectiveness of plan by outcome, making adjustments if necessary.

Allow plenty of time for the plan take effect. It may take 10, 25, or 45 instances of discipline to get results. You can make changes and adjustments based upon progress (or lack of progress).

Remember:

Careful planing and consistency — not anger and emotion — will make attempts at discipline successful.

Worksheet 1

1. *Responsible Behaviors to be Improved*

_____   _____

_____   _____

_____   _____

_____   _____

2. *Problem Behaviors to be Reduced*

_____   _____

_____   _____

_____   _____

_____   _____

3. *Priority Behaviors to Work On (taken from 1 and 2 above)*

_____

_____

_____

Worksheet 2

Increasing
Good Behavior

Positive Reinforcement

1. Praise & Encouragement
2. Activity Reinforcers
3. Material Reinforcers
4. Token Reinforcers
5. Modeling
6. Practice
7. Self-Monitoring
8. Humor

Avoidance Reinforcement

1. First Things First Principle
2. Hot Seat Approach
3. Group Effort Approach
4. Gotcha Game

Reducing
Misbehavior

Negative Consequences

1. Natural Consequences
2. Logical Consequences
3. Overcorrection
4. Positive Practice
5. Isolation
6. Response-Cost
7. Withdrawal of Privilege

Incentive Removal

1. Broken Record
2. Planned Ignoring
3. Time Out
4. Redirection/Distraction
5. Prevention
6. Reinforce Opposite Behaviors
7. Avoiding Accidental Reinforcement

For Further Reading . . .

Canter, Lee & Lee Hausner (1987). *Homework Without Tears: A Parent's Guide for Motivating Children to Do Homework and to Succeed in School.* New York: Harper & Row.

> The title says it all. Every parent should have this!

McCarney, Stephen & Angela M. Bauer (1989). *A Parent's Guide: Solutions to Today's Most Common Behavior Problems in the Home.* Colombia, MO: Hawthorne Educational Services.

> This is a "cookbook" approach, listing a wide variety of problems most parents face, and giving many possible solutions to each problem. Unfortunately, this book cannot be ordered through bookstores, but is available either directly through Hawthorne Educational Services at (800) 542-1673, or from Casey & Kirsch Publishers (see below).

Garber, Stephen W., Marianne Daniels Garber, & Robyn Freedman Spizman (1987). *Good Behavior: Over 1,200 Sensible Solutions to Your Child's Problems from Birth to Age Twelve.* New York: St. Martin's Press.

> This is also a "cookbook" approach which gives fewer ideas than *A Parent's Guide* (see above), but spends more time explaining the ideas it gives. An excellent resource to turn to when there's a problem you can't figure out.

These books can be ordered from most any bookstore
(except *A Parent's Guide*) or through:

Casey & Kirsch Publishers
(800) 331-5397

Notes